RONSARD AND DU BELLAY

VERSUS BEZE

MALCOLM C. SMITH

RONSARD & DU BELLAY VERSUS BEZE

Allusiveness in Renaissance Literary Texts

LIBRAIRIE DROZ
11, rue Massot
GENÈVE
1995

NOTE

Malcolm Smith died of cancer on 26 October 1994 at the age of 53. He had completed this book a few weeks earlier, returning to a subject that had preoccupied him as a young scholar, and drawing on his own writings since that time. He supplied the title a few days before his death. The text as he left it required light editing but it is otherwise unchanged.

MJH

Book design and typesetting by Philip Taylor, Royal Holloway and Bedford New College, University of London, based on an original design by Librairie Droz. Typeset using TₑX at the Computer Centre (RHBNC) in Adobe Times Roman 9pt and 10 pt, and processed on the Linotronic 300 of the University of London Computer Centre.

ISBN 2-600-00099-2   —

CONTENTS

Introduction   7

I: The kinship of Ronsard and Bèze   11

II: Bèze the Christian poet   17

III: Concessions   33

IV: Reconciliation?   49

V: 'Ce guerrier de Baize'   61

VI: Bèze's continuing salvoes   79

Notes   91

Bibliography 129

Introduction

For forty years, a feud raged between the greatest poet of the
French Renaissance and one of the leading French Reformers.
The poet is Ronsard, the Reformer is Théodore de Bèze; and
the initial and principal issue which divided them is whether
it is legitimate for the poet to draw inspiration from classical
pagan authors rather than from the Bible. Some of the finest
writers of the time entered the fray in support of one or other of
the two main protagonists. Two episodes in this long-running
confrontation are fairly well known: Bèze's attack on Ronsard
in 1550 in the preface to his edifying biblical play, *Abraham
sacrifiant,* and Ronsard's attack on Bèze in 1562 for preaching
a 'gospel of arms' in the first civil war. But what is not known
is that these were simply two episodes in an enduring dispute.
The encounter between Ronsard and Bèze sheds light on the
attitudes of the two of them and of their respective friends
towards the widening religious division; on the activities of a
group of conciliatory thinkers (often referred to as *moyenneurs*)
who sought to bridge the religious divide; and on the views on
poetry held by the opposing parties (and, I suspect, their views
on theological discourse as well). A first purpose of this little
book is to present the texts in which Bèze and Ronsard and
their friends confront each other.

There is another issue on which this investigation sheds
light, and an engrossing one, and it is the habit, so dear to
Renaissance writers of invective, of referring to their targets

obliquely. While they attack each other pitilessly, they often do so without naming names. It was the sheer pleasure of identifying the targets of allusive attack which led me to write this little book. When Ronsard, Bèze and others veiled the identity of their targets they made their allusions all the more pointed — and created an aura of collusion between themselves and their audience. This book invites you to venture into that conspiratorial world — and to gain, in the process, an intimate acquaintance with Ronsard, Bèze and their respective allies. For, when they write this way, they are inviting us, their unseen readers (even those separated from them by four centuries!) to enter into a relationship of intellectual and personal kinship with them, and to see at close hand how their minds worked. A second purpose of this book, then, is to explore this culture of veiled allusion.

The fact that Ronsard and Bèze usually refrained from naming each other explains why their feud has not attracted attention in modern times. But there is another reason: while Ronsard and Bèze plainly had a substantial common readership in their own day, this is no longer the case. On the whole, Ronsard has attracted the attention of historians of literature while Théodore de Bèze has been studied by historians of the Reformation. The history of literature and the history of the Reformation have largely been pursued in isolation from each other. But, arguably, this has been unscholarly: all the Pléiade poets sought in one way or another to exert an influence on the religious opinions of their contemporaries. And Bèze, besides being a great Reformer, was also a celebrated poet, and was convinced that poetry could serve theological ends. Thus, both Ronsard and Bèze saw close links between poetry and theology (though, as we shall see, different sorts of links). A third purpose of this book is to explore this issue. Today, most European poets no longer seek to expound the ways of God to men, and most European theologians no longer teach 'poetically' in parables. In the Renaissance, the divorce between poetry and theology had not yet happened.

Broadly, we shall see six phases in the relationship between Ronsard and Bèze: (i) a period of kinship (1547 – 1550), in which some close affinities between the two can be shown to have existed; (ii) a time of debate about Christian poetry, advocated by Bèze in the preface to his *Abraham* (1550) and by others in subsequent years; (iii) a period in which Ronsard and Du Bellay made concessions to this view (1552 and subsequently); (iv) a moment of apparent *rapprochement* between the two sides (1559 – 1560); (v) the first civil war (1560 – 1563) and the definitive parting of the ways; (vi) continued salvoes from Bèze and his followers up to the time of Ronsard's death in 1585, and rejoinders to them by the poet's admirers.

For the sake of brevity, I have quoted only sparingly from Ronsard, whose poems are readily available: many of the passages are magnificent invective (Bèze unintentionally inspired some of Ronsard's most vigorous lines). Also for the sake of brevity, I have tried to keep the focus firmly on Bèze and the Pléiade poets (and, where relevant, their close associates); it would have been possible, though questionably relevant, to multiply references to the debate on Christian versus pagan poetry (which of course did not begin in the sixteenth century). However, I have referred occasionally in passing to some wider issues which the subject of this book raises.

CHAPTER I

The kinship of Ronsard and Bèze

(i) Bèze and the young Pléiade

The probable first point of contact between Bèze and the embryonic Pléiade was the poet and mathematician Jacques Peletier. Peletier, a secretary of the Bishop of Le Mans, René Du Bellay, almost certainly met Ronsard in 1543 when Ronsard went to Le Mans to begin his career as a cleric by receiving the tonsure from the Bishop (1). Peletier noted in the chapter on the ode in his *Art poëtique* that Ronsard met him in Le Mans in his youth and showed him odes he had written, and told him that he was writing this kind of poetry in emulation of Horace; Peletier added that since then, Ronsard had published odes based on Horace, and also (and especially) odes which emulated those of Pindar. He noted, too, that Ronsard was the first person to use the word 'ode' in French (2).

A mutual respect and close intellectual kinship arose between Peletier and Ronsard, as is clear from a letter to Ronsard which Peletier published in 1557 in his book on Euclid: 'You know the high opinion I have always had of you, Ronsard. And I know that the view you have of me is not a low one. For we have handed posterity a memorial of our friendship by our mutual expressions of esteem, and this, indeed, is of no mean significance even while we are living: for that public confirmation has about it a certain unique delightfulness. I am very

11

keen (as I think you are) that posterity should know that we are bound together not just being contemporaries of each other, but by a union of soul... You know how great was the common accord and kinship of our minds some time back, at the time when a third scholar, Joachim Du Bellay, joined our number. I recall how in the name of the Muses, you showed such kind respect to me, your elder by a few years, when you were still a youth' (3).

That passage indicates that Peletier also had a close relationship with Joachim Du Bellay. It is probable that Peletier met Du Bellay, too, at Le Mans in 1543 (4). His relationship with Du Bellay appears to have been every bit as cordial as his relationship with Ronsard. Du Bellay noted in the preface to *L'Olive* that it was Peletier who persuaded him to write sonnets and odes, types of poetry not commonly written at that time (four years ago) in France (5). Du Bellay's first published work was a poem in Peletier's *Œuvres poëtiques* of 1547 (6). He also seems to have adopted some of Peletier's ideas in the *Deffence et illustration de la langue françoyse* (7). And he dedicated three sonnets of *Les Regrets* to him (nos. 78, 156, 189).

Shortly after making the acquaintance of Ronsard and Du Bellay, Peletier abandoned his post of rector of the Collège de Bayeux so as to devote himself more single-mindedly to a life of scholarship. In the company of a friend and fellow-scholar, Jean Martin, he went to live in the house of the printer Michel de Vascosan in the rue Saint-Jacques in Paris. Unencumbered by any professional responsibilities, he appears to have devoted the winter of 1547–48 to work on various publications (the *Œuvres poëtiques,* the *Dialogue de l'ortografe,* the *Aritmetique,* and a collection of essays in which he appears to have had a hand, the *Discours non plus melancoliques que divers*). He also seems to have spent time discussing intellectual issues, long into the night, with his friends. Into this group, Peletier welcomed Théodore de Bèze, 'a man happy in the gifts of grace, nature and fortune' (8). Vascosan's house is probably where Ronsard and Bèze first met. For Peletier's *Œuvres poëtiques,* published in September 1547 by Vascosan, contain the first published works of Ronsard (and, as we have just seen, of Du Bellay), and Vascosan was to issue several of Ronsard's earliest publications (9).

A common cultural purpose seems to have united Bèze, Ronsard, Peletier and other scholar-poets. They all sought renown as poets — and as poets who had successfully assimilated the work of their great classical predecessors, and could aspire to a status rivalling theirs. The poets in the Vascosan circle practised the same genres as the ancient poets, and wrote on similar themes. Bèze's *Poemata,* published for the first time by Conrad Badius in Paris in mid-July 1548, have been summarized as being predominantly 'Liminary verses, *silvæ,* birthday poems, translations and adaptations of poems from the *Greek Anthology,* epitaphs both serious and humorous, epithalamia, love elegies and epigrams in the Ovidian manner, and Catullan and Martialian epigrams' (10); the same description would encompass a very large part of the output of Ronsard and Du Bellay also. As Du Bellay compiled the first French collection of love sonnets in praise of his Olive, Bèze was extolling his Candida; indeed, just as Du Bellay and (especially) Ronsard were to be criticised for writing poetry which was erotic or licentious, so too was Bèze on the strength of the poems dedicated to Candida in the collection of 1548. And though Du Bellay, Ronsard and Peletier generally wrote in French while Bèze's poetry was in Latin, this difference was a superficial and transient one: Ronsard's first work had been in Latin, and Du Bellay was to become a great Latin poet, while Bèze was shortly to publish poetry in French.

In some of his early poems, Ronsard seems to have drawn inspiration from Bèze (11). There are also possible echoes of Bèze in Du Bellay (12). And in the *Poematum libri quatuor,* Du Bellay was to include Bèze in a list of famous contemporary love poets (13).

(ii) The obscurantism of the Sorbonne

We shall see later, when we look at a famous letter to Melchior
Volmar which Bèze published in 1560, that Bèze already had
some contact with the views of the Reformers at the time he
met Peletier, and had been tempted to adopt those views. He
appears however at this time to have refrained from telling his
friends about this. However, if he did, Ronsard, Peletier and Du
Bellay are not likely to have been discountenanced by any radical opinions he may have proffered. All three were animated
by scholarly openness; all three had an attitude towards the
prevailing wisdoms which bordered on the iconoclastic. The
tracts on which Peletier was working sought radical reform
of orthography and mathematics, and Ronsard and Du Bellay,
in their manifestos, insisted time and again on what separated
them from their predecessors.

More specifically, all these poets seem also to have had in
common an aversion for what they saw as the obscurantism
of the Sorbonne. Some years later, Estienne Pasquier was to
declare in his *Recherches de la France* that Bèze and Peletier
were (with Maurice Scève) the vanguard in a war against ignorance — and, Pasquier added, Ronsard and Du Bellay followed
close behind in this endeavour (14). Pasquier was echoing
Ronsard's denunciations of the 'vilain monstre Ignorance', and
both Pasquier and Ronsard seem to have been attacking the
Sorbonne and its opposition to the study of Greek and Hebrew
and to publication of the Bible (15).

In the expanded edition of *L'Olive,* which appeared in
1550, Du Bellay included a long polemical poem, *La Musa-
gnœomachie,* or 'battle of the Muses and of Ignorance', which
projects the same sentiment. The monster, benighted and cruel,
seems to represent the Sorbonne; and as enemies of the monster, Du Bellay presents (in addition to poets) men who were
to acquire a strong reputation for scholarship and for openness
to new ideas — François Olivier, Pierre Du Chastel, Jean de
Monluc and Pierre Danès (16).

Revealingly, Bèze and Du Bellay had a common view on a contemporary *cause célèbre,* the execution in August 1546 of Estienne Dolet. Of all people, Dolet best epitomized the hostility of scholars to the obscurantism of the Sorbonne; and, unlike others, he sustained that opposition *jusques au feu inclusivement.* Bèze deplored Dolet's death in his *Poemata* of 1548 (17); and Du Bellay, in the *Deffence et illustration* of 1549, extolled Dolet's memory — and, not content with praising a man whose biblical publications had been condemned by the Sorbonne and who had been burned (with his books) for his opinions, he castigated the 'crass ignorance' of the 'venerable Druids' of the Sorbonne who oppose vernacular Bibles; and he expressed the hope that Dolet's unpublished book on rhetoric will see the light of day (18) (prudently, the young poet dedicated the *Deffence* to his father's cousin, Cardinal Jean Du Bellay, whose protection, as he noted in the dedicatory letter, would be a shield and protection for him). The kinship between Bèze and Du Bellay on the question of Dolet is all the more remarkable in that Dolet had been abandoned, and publicly, by almost all his humanist friends.

There is no obvious reason why Bèze on the one hand and Ronsard and Du Bellay on the other should have parted company on religion. Indeed, Bèze hesitated for a long time before adopting the Reformation (19). Ronsard and Du Bellay, for their part, deplored that corruption in the Catholic Church which drove so many into the arms of the Reformers, and which remained painfully uncorrected. In one of the odes published in 1550, Ronsard attacked what he called 'fraudes rommaines' (20); and Du Bellay's comments on clerical corruption, found notably but by no means exclusively in *Les Regrets,* are well known (21). Indeed, Ronsard seems to have had some interest in the doctrines of the Reformers, for he was to note later that he had, in his youth, 'tasted the poisoned honey' of the Reformers (22). Thus, Bèze and the two leading poets in the group which was to become known as the Pléiade were probably a lot closer in 1548 — culturally, intellectually and even on religion — than either side was prepared to admit later.

(iii) The parting of the ways

Within months of the (probable) first acquaintance of Bèze and
the three poets who could be described as the Pléiade in em-
bryo, this group of young humanist-poets was broken up. Even
as his friendship with Peletier deepened, Bèze was being torn
in different directions. On the one hand, he was delighted by
the literary life of Paris and by his growing reputation as a poet,
and was gratified by the income which came with the ecclesiastical benefices his relatives gave him; on the other hand,
he had determined a decade earlier to follow his mentor, the
Reformer Melchior Volmar, who had taught him in Orléans and
Bourges from 1528 to 1535, to Germany, and he had secretly
promised to marry Catherine Denosse (23). He was to evoke
these tensions years later, as we shall see, in his famous letter
to Volmar. Bèze left Paris in October 1548 — for Geneva, and
as a religious refugee. A contemporary, Nicolas de Nicolaï, attributed his flight to the composition of his epigram in defence
of Dolet: 'I hear he has fled from France to Switzerland, but
I do not know what precipitated his flight. However, I suspect
that he incurred odium for that epigram in which he extols Dolet, an atheist who was convicted and burned in Paris. If only
he had not published that epigram!' (24). At all events, the
Paris *Parlement* put him on trial as a fugitive Reformer and,
on 31 May 1550, sentenced him to be burned in effigy (25). In
the meantime, Peletier had left Paris by mid-September 1548,
first for Bordeaux and then Poitiers. The reason for his departure is obscure, but the likeliest explanation is that he feared
religious persecution (26).

CHAPTER II

Bèze the Christian poet

(i) Biblical or secular models?

Bèze seems first to have fallen out with Ronsard and Du Bellay over the question of whether a poet should seek inspiration in the Bible or in secular models. In fact, all three were to become 'biblical' poets, and there was little difference between them in substance. Moreover, it was only by accident that this first dispute arose at all. The dispute would hardly be worth looking at were it not that it triggered a long-running feud of great historical interest. To understand the genesis of this first dispute, it is necessary to recall the circumstances in which Ronsard and Du Bellay published their first collections of poems, in 1549 and 1550.

Their poetry, inspired by years of careful study and assimilation of classical models, met with a number of objections, one of which was (as recorded by Du Bellay) that 'Marot n'a point ainsi ecrit' (27). That this objection was made is indeed understandable: both Ronsard and Du Bellay sought to supplant Clément Marot, the most illustrious of their predecessors. Thus, for example, Ronsard dismissed him in the preface to his *Odes* (the book was published in February or March 1550), as the 'seulle lumiere *en ses ans* de la vulgaire poësie' — implying he no longer enjoyed this status. And when Ronsard referred to what he called the 'foible et languissante' poetry which pre-

17

ceded his own and that of Du Bellay, he condescendingly ex-
cepted Scève, Heroët and Saint-Gelais from this condemnation, but not Marot. Further, he began an ode in celebration of
François de Bourbon's victory at Ceresole by saying Marot's
poem on the same subject was not good enough, that it was a
mere amateurish outline (28).

More precisely, and more relevantly to us, Marot was famous pre-eminently for his translations of the psalms, which
had first appeared in 1541 (29). It was acknowledged — and
by an observer as close to the Pléiade as Jacques Peletier — that
Marot's psalm translations were odes in all but name (30). But
Ronsard sought above all else in these years to be known as the
inventor of the ode. He is the 'premier auteur lirique françois',
and has chosen a 'sentier inconnu pour aller à l'immortalité',
as he put it in the preface to the *Odes* of 1550 (31); his poems
are 'nouvelles inventions', a 'musique toute neuve', they are
new emulations of ancient poets whom no-one has previously
been able to imitate; he is following a 'nouvelle trace' (32).
Repeatedly, he claimed to have invented the ode, that is, to be
the person who first successfully introduced this ancient lyri-
cal genre into French (33). But surely — as Peletier acknowledged — Marot had some claim to have preceded Ronsard in
the composition of what were effectively odes? Ronsard met
this objection by claiming in his preface to the *Odes* that he
had begun writing these poems a long while ago, at the time
when Marot was working on his psalm translations.

Ronsard was not content to assert that he (and not Marot)
was the innovator. He stressed an important difference between
himself and Marot. Marot, in a prefatory poem in his psalms,
had stressed that his model was biblical: he had compared Horace to King David and found him wanting (34). Ronsard, on
the other hand, truculently declared that his own model was
Horace (35). Meantime, Du Bellay, who was publishing odes
of his own in 1549 and who was no more willing than Ronsard
to take second place to Marot, disparaged Marot's psalm translations in the *Deffence et illustration de la langue françoys,* also
of 1549. There, he observed caustically that some people claim

to translate from languages of which they are ignorant — an allusion to Marot, who had claimed his translation of the psalms was based on 'la verité hebraïque' (36). Ronsard and Du Bellay were clearly both keen to disparage Marot and his most famous work, but in attacking a translation of the psalms and in commending a secular model they exposed themselves to the charge that their writing was 'pagan'.

(ii) Bèze's first attack

This background helps us understand Bèze's position. His conversion to the Reformed faith led him to renounce rapidly his earlier view that the poet should seek inspiration in classical models, and he was to devote himself to producing edifying verse, notably translations of the psalms, first into French verse and later into Latin verse. And he sought to distance himself vigorously from the friends who had shared his enthusiasm for classical literature. This we see in the preface (dated 1 October 1550) to his edifying biblical play, *Abraham sacrifiant:*

> [. . .] Que pleust à Dieu que tant de bons espriz que je cognoy en France, en lieu de s'amuser à ces malheureuses inventions ou imitations de fantaisies vaines et deshonnestes (si on en veult juger à la verité), regardassent plustost à magnifier la bonté de ce grand Dieu, duquel ils ont receu tant de graces, qu'à flatter leurs idoles, c'est à dire leurs seigneurs ou leurs dames, qu'ils entretiennent en leurs vices par leurs fictions et flatteries. A la verité il leur seroit mieux seant de chanter un cantique à Dieu que de petrarquiser un sonnet et faire l'amoureux transy, digne d'avoir un chapperon à sonnettes, ou de contrefaire ces fureurs poëtiques à l'antique, pour distiller la gloire de ce monde, et immortaliser cestuy cy ou ceste là, choses qui font confesser au lecteur que les autheurs d'icelles n'ont pas seulement monté en leur mont de Parnasse, mais sont parvenuz jusques au cercle de la Lune. Les autres (du nombre desquels j'ay esté à mon tresgrand regret) esguissent un epigramme trenchant à deux costez ou picquant par le bout, les

> autres s'amusent à tout renverser plutost qu'à tourner, autres cuidans enrichir nostre langue, l'accoustrent à la Grecque et à la Romaine. [. . .] Mesmes j'ay faict un cantique hors le chorus, et n'ay usé de strophes, antistrophes, epirremes, parecbases, ny autres tels mots qui ne servent que d'espoventer les simples gens [. . .] (37).

Bèze has two targets in this passage. The person who 'petrarchises a sonnet and acts as a lover in a trance' is Joachim Du Bellay who, in 1549, published *L'Olive* and who, in that collection of love sonnets, had claimed ostentatiously to be an emulator of Petrarch (38). Such a person, says Bèze, deserves to have a hood with bells on it — the attribute, then, of a fool (39). Du Bellay was stung into a pointed riposte, as we shall see. Many denunciations by Reformers of the love poetry of the Pléiade were to follow.

Secondly, Bèze's preface attacks Ronsard, whose *Odes* (published earlier in 1550 but written over a period of several years beforehand and undoubtedly circulated in manuscript to acquaintances) introduced the Greek metric divisions (strophes and antistrophes) into France. Ronsard also laid emphasis on the 'fureurs poëtiques à l'antique' which Bèze decries. And Bèze's attack on poets who make 'idols' of those they flatter recalls Ronsard's compliments to notable contemporaries, compliments which were indeed (as he acknowledged) hyperbolic: he had 'deified' Henri II in the first poem of the first book of *Odes* of 1550 and was to continue to use such hyperbole (40). Again, denunciations of the 'flattery' found in the poetry of the Pléiade were to be numerous in the years that followed.

A little later in the preface, Bèze attacks a third person:

> Quant à l'orthographie, j'ay voulu que l'imprimeur suyvit la commune, quelques maigres fantaisies qu'on ait mis en avant depuis trois ou quatre ans en ça, et conseillerois volontiers aux plus opiniastres de ceux qui l'ont changée (s'ils estoyent gens qui demandassent conseil à autres qu'à eux mesmes), puis qu'ils la veulent ranger selon la prononciation, c'est à dire puis qu'ils veulent faire qu'il y ait quasi autant de manieres d'escrire qu'il

y a non seulement de contrées, mais aussi de personnes
en France, ils apprenent à prononcer devant que vouloir
apprendre à escrire: car (pour parler et escrire à leur
façon) celuy n'est pas dinne de balher les regles d'escrire
noutre langue, qui ne la peut parler.

This refers to Peletier's *Dialogue de l'ortografe* — where, precisely, Peletier presents Bèze as a defender of the conservative
position on orthography (and Bèze's spellings 'dinne' and 'balher' are parodies of reforms Peletier advocated) (41). Peletier
might also be in part the target of the attack on Petrarchists
in the earlier passage we have looked at, for he had translated
twelve of Petrarch's sonnets into French (42). And he may be
the butt of the attack on those who claim to enrich the French
language: for Peletier had urged doing this in an ode *A un poète
qui n'escrivoit qu'en latin,* an ode which may itself have been
addressed to Bèze (43). The preface to *Abraham* is, so far as
is known, Bèze's one and only allusion to Peletier, the close
friend of the winter of 1547 – 48; and it is curious that it should
be hostile. Perhaps Bèze wanted to cast a veil over the years in
which he had been writing the *Poemata* and over his links with
the early Pléiade. Peletier, on the other hand, continued for a
while to extol Bèze (44), and seems to have had no qualms
about divulging his association with him (45).

Thus, immediately after his conversion, Bèze turned his
back on his earlier friends. There is evidence, which Natalie
Davis has rehearsed, that Peletier was distressed by this abrupt
about-turn; and we shall see that some years later, Ronsard
was to deplore the departure of Bèze from France. Another
immediate consequence of Bèze's conversion (for consequence
it must have been) was that he dropped from his poems that
charming epitaph of Dolet which so eloquently ranked him
among the partisans of intellectual freedom (46); and a further
consequence is his decision to translate the psalms into French.

For Bèze announces in that same preface to *Abraham* that
he has turned his energies to translating the psalms. Much
later, in 1579, in his summary of Psalm 91, he was to recall
how, thirty-one years earlier, when he had left his homeland

and given up his possessions to serve Christ in freedom, he had attended a public Christian service for the first time and, hearing Psalm 91 sung, had felt fortified, as though God himself were addressing him (47). And so, in 1550, when Bèze began translating the psalms, he was continuing the work of Clément Marot — and implicitly separating himself further from the 'pagan' poetry of Ronsard and Du Bellay.

It was at the urging of Calvin that Bèze started translating the psalms (48). When Calvin first came to Geneva, in January 1537, he had noted that 'C'est une chose bien expediente à l'édification de l'esglise de chanter aulcungs pseaumes en forme d'oraysons publicqs'; this preoccupation had been strengthened in 1539 by his experience of the liturgy in the German church in Strasbourg; in that year, he published in Strasbourg thirteen psalm translations by Marot (whom he had almost certainly met in 1536 in Ferrara) in a compilation titled *Aulcuns pseaulmes et cantiques mys en chant*; and from that date, compilations in which Marot's translations were complemented by liturgical pieces by Calvin appeared regularly (49). Already in 1551, thirty-four of Bèze's psalm translations were to appear in a volume alongside forty-nine of Marot's, and by 1562 the Calvinist psalter was complete (50).

(iii) Du Bellay replies to Bèze

Du Bellay was stung by Bèze's denunciation, in the preface to *Abraham,* of his love sonnets. His anger was doubtless all the more acute in that Bèze had ignored the underlying theological content of *L'Olive.* For while at first sight the collection celebrates the poet's love for a person called Olive (whom some historians have tried, quite unconvincingly, to identify), the collection is also — and primarily — a theological meditation, celebrating the reconciliation of God and man. The olive, Du Bellay recalls at the beginning and end of his collection, is a biblical symbol of this reconciliation (see sonnets 5 and 107); and his love story begins on Christmas Day and ends on Good Friday, thereby corresponding to the life of Christ; and the work is full of other biblical allusions. No commentator (so far as I know) has pointed to this theological dimension to the collection (51). However, in the sixteenth century, in a society better attuned than ours both to Judaeo-Christian theology and to allusive discourse, these facts about the work must have been obvious: so Bèze's dismissal of *L'Olive* as a mere human love story would certainly have rankled with Du Bellay.

Du Bellay hit back very vigorously. His rejoinder has passed unnoticed, however, and this is because Du Bellay, as was his wont, spared the name of the target of his invective (52). The relevant poem is his *Ode au Seigneur Des Essars, sur le discours de son Amadis,* published in 1552 (it was republished in 1560, with the *Monomachie de David et de Goliath*). My first extract from this poem is part of the passage in which Du Bellay defends the translation by Herberay Des Essarts of part of the *Amadis* series of novels (53):

> Vous, que les Dieux ont esleus
> Pour combatre l'ignorance,
> Et dont les escrits sont leus
> Des voisins de nostre France,
> Donnez à cestuy l'honneur,
> Qui les faict par son bonheur
> De nostre langue apprentis:
> Langue, qui estoit bornée
> Du Rhin, et du Pyrenée,
> Des Alpes, et de Thetis.
>
> Peut-estre aussi, que les ans,
> Après un long et long aage,
> Par estrangers courtisans
> Brouilleront nostre langage:
> Adonques la purité
> De sa doulce gravité
> Se pourra trouver icy,
> Du Grec la veine feconde,
> Et la Romaine faconde
> Revivent encor' ainsi.

In my second extract, Du Bellay deplores the proliferation of attacks on poetry:

> [...] ces graves enseigneurs
> D'une effrontée asseurance
> Se prennent aux grands Seigneurs,
> Les accusant d'ignorance.
> Mesmes leurs cler-voyans yeux
> Se monstrent tant curieux,
> Que d'abaisser leurs edicts
> Jusqu'aux simples damoiselles,
> Et aux cabinetz de celles,
> Qui lisent nostre Amadis.
>
> Si le Harpeur ancien,
> Qui perdit deux fois sa femme,
> Corrompit l'air Thracien
> D'une furieuse flamme:
> Pourtant nous n'avons appris
> D'avoir l'amour à mespris,
> Dont la saincte ardeur nous poingt,
> Non celle desnaturée,
> Qui de Venus ceinturée
> Les loix ne recognoist point.
>
> Mais pourquoy se sent blessé
> Par nostre façon d'escrire
> Celuy, qui a tout laissé
> Fors son vice de mesdire?
> Lequel pour se deffacher,
> Voulant (ce semble) attacher
> Or' cestuy, ores celuy,
> Par ne sçay quelles sornettes
> Fait un present de sonnettes,
> A qui est moins fol que luy (54).

This is the culmination to a passage on enemies of poetry, the worst enemy being this person who 'Fait un present de sonnettes': and that is Bèze who, in *Abraham,* had castigated the Petrarchist fool (Du Bellay) who was 'digne d'avoir un chapperon à sonnettes'. To help ensure his reader gets the allusion, Du Bellay describes his target earlier in the stanza as 'Celuy, qui a tout laissé' — a reference to Bèze's departure from France. And conceivably, in the preceding stanza about the *Amadis* novels being defensible as they celebrate a love that is heterosexual, Du Bellay is insinuating, as others were to do, that the Reformer was a homosexual (55).

Did Du Bellay also attack Bèze in *Les Regrets*? He there berates an assortment of enemies: 'Sur les vers je vomis le venin de mon cœur' (sonnet 14). Conceivably, sonnet 65 alludes to Bèze: the culminating tercet attacks the unnamed foe for homosexuality, for atheism (Bèze's Christian name invited parallels with the ancient atheist Theodore (56)), and for being a pedant (Bèze was a professor at Lausanne). In sonnet 136, Du Bellay notes he has passed through Geneva (though he does not name the city and invites us to recognize it by his unflattering description), but nothing there points specifically to Bèze — nor does anything in his five further sonnets which reply to a Reformer who objected to sonnet 136 (57).

(iv) Ronsard replies to Bèze

Ronsard, for his part, also replied to Bèze's preface to *Abraham*. In the long ode dedicated to Michel de L'Hospital and published in 1553, he has Jupiter warn the Muses that inspired poets are going to be attacked as *furieux*:

> Ceux là que je feindrai Poétes
> Par la grace de ma bonté,
> Seront nommez les Interpretes
> Des Dieux, et de leur volonté:
> Mais ilz seront tout au contraire
> Appellez sotz, et furieux,
> Par le caquet du populaire
> Mechantement injurieux.
> Tousjours pendra devant leur face
> Quelque Demon, qui au besoing
> Diligentement aura soing
> De toutes choses qu'on leur face (58).

Bèze had mocked Ronsard's claim to 'contrefaire ces fureurs poëtiques à l'antique', and this passage is doubtless Ronsard's rejoinder.

And in the second book of *Hymnes* of 1556:

> Encore je voudrois que le doux Simonide
> (Pourveu qu'il ne pleurast), Alcman et Bacchylide,
> Alcée, et Stesichore, et ces neuf chantres Grecs
> Fussent ressuscités: nous les lirions exprès
> Pour choisir leurs beaux vers pleins de douces parolles,
> Et les graves seroient pour les maistres d'escolles,
> Affin d'espouvanter les simples escoliers
> Au bruit de ces gros vers furieux et guerriers (59).

The declared aim, 'espouvanter les simples escoliers', echoes the phrase in Bèze's preface to *Abraham,* 'espovanter les simples gens'.

(v)   Bèze's second attack

In a poem published in a 1553 edition of the psalms, Bèze underlined his divergence from Ronsard — although again without naming him. He also renewed his denunciation of flattering poets who present court dignitaries as 'gods':

> Sus donc, esprits de celeste origine,
> Monstrez icy votre fureur divine,
> Et ceste grace autant peu imitable
> Au peuple bas, qu'aux plus grands admirable.
> Soyent desormais voz plumes adonnées
> A louer Dieu, qui les vous a données.
> C'est trop servi à ses affections,
> C'est trop suivy folles inventions.
> On a beau faire et complaintes et criz,
> Dames mourront, et vous, et voz escrits!
> Flattez, mentez, faites du diable un ange,
> Vos dieux mourront, vous et vostre louange.
> Reveillez vous, amis, de vostre songe,
> Et m'embrassez verité pour mensonge.
> Ne permettez, gentilles creatures,
> Vos beaux esprits croppir en ces ordures,

Cercher vous faut ailleurs qu'en ce bas monde
Dignes sujets de vostre grand'faconde.
Mais pour ce faire, il faut premierement
Que reformiez voz cœurs entierement.
Voz plumes lors, d'un bon esprit poussées,
Descouvriront voz divines pensées.
Lors serez vous poëtes veritables,
Prisés des bons, aux meschans redoutables.
Sinon, chantez voz feintes poësies,
Dames, amours, complaintes, jalousies.
Quant est de moy, tout petit que je suis,
Je veux louer mon Dieu comme je puis [. . .] (60).

This passage neatly sums up the principal objections of Bèze, and many of his friends, to the poetry of Ronsard: it deals with love, it is pagan, and it is obsequious towards the mighty. The expression 'faire d'un diable un ange' is biblical and was proverbial (61). Ronsard saw himself, with undoubted reason, as the target of this passage: as we shall see later, he published a rejoinder to it.

(vi) Supporters of Bèze

The views Bèze expresses on poetry in the preface to *Abraham* and in the 1551 edition of the psalms were to be influential. Interestingly, that influence can be seen in poets who were themselves friends or emulators of Ronsard.

Estienne Jodelle is one. Jodelle may have read Bèze's preface to *Abraham*; he may have seen the play performed in Lausanne (for he was in Switzerland around 1550) (62). He published in the second half of 1551 an epigram saying that Bèze had suffered from the plague when translating the psalms and that the reason the plague had assaulted Bèze was that in translating the psalms, 'Beze assailloit la peste à tous mortelle' (63). Clearly, Jodelle was at this time a Reformer (64).

Together with this epigram, Jodelle published a sonnet in praise of Bèze's translation of the psalms, and it shows Jodelle siding with Bèze against the 'pagan' poets of the day:

Bien que fuyans par la celeste trace,
Croyez au vol du cheval de voz cieulx
Pour estonner l'aureille de voz dieux
Des vieux fredons de la lirique grace;

Bien que feigniez (armez de docte audace)
Ne craindre point le passaige oublieux,
Bien qu'effaciez de traictz delicieux
Le noir oubly qui voz amys efface;

Cil qui sonnant soubz ce prince ancien,
Quittant le son tebain et tracien,
De Jésus Christ la troupe va duisant,

Plus que vous tous de loz a merité
Espérant bien plus seure eternité
Ayant pour but le seul eternisant (65).

This sonnet is far from lucid! Pagan poets (Jodelle says) are conveyed on the back of the winged horse Pegasus and swept up to heaven where they impress the pagan gods with classically-inspired verse; and they claim to have no fear of oblivion, as their work confers immortality on them and on those they extol. Bèze, by contrast, emulates King David, shuns the style of Thebes (Pindar) and of Thrace (Orpheus), offers guidance to the flock of Christ, deserves greater praise than all the latter-day pagans and has as his goal the immortality which comes from God and which God alone can grant.

A little later, in a preliminary poem published with the *Cantiques* of Nicolas Denisot, Jodelle returned to the attack:

Fuyons ces vois menteresses,
Que nous servent ces Déesses [. . .]
Si cette seule victoire
De Jesuchrist est ma gloire [. . .] (66)

Jodelle was not the only contributor to this collection to renounce 'pagan' poetry and extol Christian verse. Incidentally, Jodelle's sympathy for the Reformation was to be short-lived: he was later to become a strident defender of the Catholic faith (67) and foe of Bèze (68) — before dying as a reputed atheist (69).

Another poet who echoed Bèze is Jean Tagaut, a friend and colleague of Bèze's at Lausanne, where he taught mathematics (70). Tagaut was influenced by Ronsard's *Odes* when writing his own, between 1550 and 1552 (71). Notwithstanding this indebtedness, Tagaut echoed the sentiments of the Reformer on pagan poetry:

> [...] Or fuy-moy tous ces Dieuz
> Que nous enfanta la Grece,
> Un seul gouverne les cieuz
> Par l'indicible sagesse
> De sa haute Providence,
> C'est l'eternelle Prudence
> Qui par sa saincte parolle
> En un clin d'œil a formé
> Le ciel et le temps qui vole (72).

It is probable that his target was the arch-exponent of pagan verse, Ronsard.

A third Reformer who attacked Ronsard was Albert Babinot. In 1554, he began work on his *Christiade* (doubtless conceived as an antidote to Ronsard's vigorously-canvassed but long-delayed *Franciade*). He knew Ronsard's *Odes*, and doubtless had Ronsard in mind when he wrote the following lines:

> Cesse, c'est trop, heureus esprit François,
> Cesse, c'est trop chanté d'une amour vaine,
> Emploie moi ceste gentile veine,
> Pour cil, lequel te donne ceste voix...
> Car c'est lui seul, qui peut salariser
> Ton saint labeur, et ta teste immortelle (73).

Babinot has been described as a Catholic, but it appears that he had been converted to the Reformation by Calvin as early as 1534 (74).

And a fourth Reformer who entered the fray against Ronsard was Accace (or Accasse) Dalbiac (or d'Albiac; also known as Du Plessis). In 1556, he published in Lausanne a collection titled *Les Proverbes de Salomon, Ensemble l'Ecclesiaste, mise en cantiques et rime françoise selon la verité hebraïque*, with music by F. Gindron. An introductory ode, *A tous chrestiens*, echoes the view that God-given talents should be deployed in praise of the Creator:

> Veu l'heureux temps où nous sommes,
> Je m'esbahi d'aucuns hommes
> Douez par le Createur
> De tant de beaux dons et graces,
> Desquels ces maudites races
> Ne recognoissent l'autheur.
>
> Je voy des braves Poëtes
> Comme nocturnes chouettes,
> Rien ne chantans que la nuict,
> Et maints esprits de haute aile,
> Desquels la plume et le zelle
> Ne sont qu'un terrestre bruit [. . .]
>
> Pour qui sont les gorges nettes,
> Lucs, violles, espinettes?
> Pour qui tous instrumens faits?
> Quoy que main d'homme les sonne,
> Si est-ce que Dieu les donne,
> Pour annoncer ses hauts faits [. . .]
>
> Mais voicy voz maladies,
> Voz doux chans, et melodies
> Ne sont enflez que d'orgueil:
> Ny voz escris admirables
> Dignes que d'hommes, ou diables,
> Ausquels vous servez à l'œil.

As has been pointed out, Accace d'Albiac's target is probably Ronsard (75).

Another Reformer, Guillaume Gueroult, declared in a prefatory poem in the *Premier livre des Pseaumes, cantiques et chansons spirituelles,* published in Geneva in 1554, that he wanted the name of God to be the 'Seul argument et discours de mon mettre'. The content of his poem is similar to that of those reviewed here, but he does not really belong in our survey of disciples of Bèze who were opposed to Ronsard. For one thing, there is no indication that this or indeed any of Gueroult's writing was directed explicitly at Ronsard. For another,

Gueroult's relationship with Calvin and Bèze became one of hostility: Gueroult's work on the psalms was seen by Calvin as usurping Bèze's own role; Gueroult himself ridiculed Bèze's translations; Bèze struck back in verse, and also complained to the Council of Geneva about the 'scandal' of the denunciation of him (76).

(vii) A mysterious attack on Ronsard and Marot

A curious anonymous work, published by the Marnef brothers in Poitiers, may be relevant to our investigation. It is titled *Discours non plus melancholiques que divers*; as we noted earlier, it seems that at least part is by Jacques Peletier; various other names have been suggested as authors (77). The work only appeared in 1556, but parts of it at least were written well before: in a foreword, Enguilbert de Marnef notes that he has published it '[...] après avoir eu long temps gardé [*sic*] cecy entre mes papiers'. And the *privilegium* is dated 7 March 1547 (that is, 1548 new style). Marnef hints that the book has several authors: '[...] je ne veus ici jurer, que tout soit d'un homme'.

Chapter 15, titled 'Le profit qu'avons des lettres et livres, et de la gloire de nos rimeurs', contains a rebuke addressed to those writers who claim immortality for their works. The author castigates ancient authors first, then turns to Christians in the following passage:

> J'endure toutesfois encores tellement quellement ceste folle esperance et ventance par trop grande en ces gens là: mais nous qui avons eu autre discipline, et veu plus que ces anciens là, devrions nous pas estre plus sages? Persisterons nous en leur folie? Que di je persister? Mais l'augmenterons? *Non possum ferre Quirites,* un tas de rimeurs de ce temps, qui amenent en nostre tant chaste France toutes les bougreries des anciens Gregeois et Latins, remplissants leurs livres d'Odes [...] de Strophe, Antistrophe, Epode et d'autres tels noms de Diables, autant à propos en nostre François, que it Magnificat à matines, mais pour dire qu'en avons ouy parler du Pindare: et ne vous sçauroient faire trois vers, qu'ils ne

> medisent d'autrui, ne se louent jusques au dernier Ciel,
> et finalement ne se croient immortelz. La Mort ni mort,
> dit l'un. L'autre R [*sic*] (78).

'La mort ni [i.e. "n'y"] mort' was the device of Clément
Marot (79). As for his other target, 'R', this is patently Ronsard, the Pindaric poet *par excellence*. And there the passage
ends, with the note 'Ce chapitre est imperfait'.

While the book did not appear until 1556, it seems likely
that this passage was written much earlier, and doubtless formed
part of the compilation for which the *privilegium* had been secured. For after Bèze's preface to *Abraham,* and even more
so after Ronsard's preface to his *Odes,* the situation was polarised: the Pléiade and their supporters attacked Marot, and the
latter's partisans attacked them, but no-one (so far as I know)
simultaneously attacked both.

Who wrote the chapter denouncing Marot and Ronsard? (80). The substance of the attack on Ronsard recalls the
attack in Bèze's preface to *Abraham.* It is tempting to specu-
late that this chapter was written by Bèze himself, especially
as Bèze (through his connection with Peletier and the Vascosan
circle) is almost certainly among the relatively small number of
people who knew, before the publication in 1550 of the *Odes,*
that Ronsard was writing Pindaric poetry; and Peletier could
have supplied the Marnefs with Bèze's views for, after spend-
ing the winter of 1547 – 48 in close discussion with Bèze, he
left for Poitiers, where he had his next works published by the
Marnefs. But Bèze is known to have admired Marot from an
early date, and so is unlikely to be the author of this attack
on him and Ronsard (81). Whoever did write this passage is
one of the first opponents of Ronsard's alleged 'paganism', as-
suming this material formed part of the book for which the
privilegium was secured in 1548; and whoever wrote it was in
full agreement with Bèze, at least in his sentiments on Ronsard.

CHAPTER III

Concessions

(i) Catholics call for edifying verse

The early confrontations between Bèze and other Reformers
on the one hand, and Ronsard and Du Bellay on the other,
might lead us to conclude that Reformers were in favour of
biblical and edifying poetry, and that Catholics were not. In
fact, the difference between the two sides was at most one of
nuance. We shall see in this chapter that both Du Bellay and
Ronsard were to write 'Christian' poetry, and that even where
their work is not explicitly edifying and biblical, it often has an
underlying meaning which the most demanding Christian critic
would endorse.

We noted that Bèze and like-minded Reformers criticised
Ronsard, broadly, on three counts: that his poetry was erotic
or licentious, that it was obsequious towards the powerful, and
that it was 'pagan' rather than Christian. Catholic critics made
precisely the same observations. Jacques Peletier denounced
love poetry in 1550 in an *Apologie à Louis Meigret* which
prefaces his *Dialogue de l'ortografe et prononciation françoise*:

> Qu'à la mienne volonté que ceus qui mettent leurs escrits
> en lumiere, fust de leur invention ou de leur traduction,
> eussent telle envie de profiter au public, comme tu te
> monstres avoir, ne t'amusant à ces communes et popu-
> laires folies, qui sont tant seulement plaisantes, ainçois

> ridicules, et de neant profitables. Entre lesquelles la plus celebre, est le sujet d'Amour, qui a esté tout un temps demené entre les François à l'envi, de telle sorte qu'à bon droit on l'a pu appeler la filosofie de France (82).

He was followed by Nicolas Denisot, whose *Cantiques* appeared at the beginning of 1553 (83). These *Cantiques* were accompanied by edifying preliminary poems, and in one of them Marc-Antoine Muret urged poets to forsake erotic verse and extol the Creator (84). Another edifying Catholic poet was the author of a collection of *Chansons tressalutaires et catholiques* of 1554 who, in the preface to his *Epitre aux lecteurs,* notes that Moses and David and 'les anciens peres' sang canticles and psalms to God, and that he hopes to inspire 'excellents Poetes' to emulate his own edifying example; he declares there, too, that his goal is to 'donner entrée aux excellentz poetes d'immiter son entreprinse, et de vous degouster des chansons pleines d'impudicitez, qui corrumpent bonnes mœurs'. A poem on the verso of the page of this collection has already set the tone:

> Armes ou amour descrire
> N'est pas mon intention.
> Je veux louer sur ma lyre
> L'eternel Dieu de Sion
> Qui des cieux où il reside
> Tire à mon esprit la bride
> Et me dit que desormais
> Il ne faut plus que je chante
> Chose lascive ou meschante
> Mais sa louange à jamais.

And one of his songs contains the following exhortation:

> Changeons propos, c'est trop chanté d'amours:
> C'est pour gens lourds, qui n'ont sens en la teste.
> Nuls bons chrestiens n'ont à Venus recours,
> Ains avec pleurs font à Dieu leur requeste (85).

Many of the songs in this collection are pious parodies of erotic songs, of a kind frequently found at the time (86).

Catholics attacked Ronsard for flattery, too, as Bèze had done. Estienne de La Boëtie may well have been thinking of Ronsard when, in the *Servitude volontaire,* he deplored hyperbolic praise of kings (and he returned to that theme in a poem, *In adulatores poetas,* which again may have been directed at Ronsard) (87). And Estienne Pasquier, in a well-known letter to the poet in 1555, urged him to moderate his eulogies:

> [...] je souhaiterois que ne fissiez si bon marché de vostre plume à hault-loüer quelques-uns que nous sçavons notoirement n'en estre dignes. Car en ce faisant, vous me direz qu'estes contraint par leurs importunitez de ce faire, ores que n'en ayez envie. Je le croy: mais la plume d'un bon poëte n'est pas telle que l'oreille d'un juge, qui doit donner de mesme balance au mauvais tout ainsi qu'au bon. Car quant à la plume du poëte, elle doit estre seulement voüée à la celebration de ceux qui le meritent (88).

Ronsard's critics were perhaps being a little unfair: it was well known at the time that such eulogies were very largely conventional — and that in extolling the holder of a given public office, the poet would often draw attention to the merits appropriate to the holder of that office, whether or not the individual actually possessed them (89).

And the criticism of paganism and advocacy of Christian verse is found in Catholic authors too. An example is Ronsard's protector Michel de L'Hospital (90). Another Catholic writer, Jean Macer, in a *Philippique contre les poëtastres et rimailleurs françois de nostre temps,* attacked Ronsard for writing pagan (and licentious) verse. Macer's denunciation actually illustrates the non-sectarian nature of this issue rather well, for he also attacked Bèze, 'ce gentil adultere, protestant, qui, par ses beaux dits, a seduit la candide femme d'un Parisien' (91). Another interesting indication that the issue was not seen in sectarian terms can be seen in the preface to Albert Babinot's *Christiade*. We saw in the last chapter that this work was doubtless conceived as a rival to Ronsard's *Franciade,* and that Babinot was a Reformer. However, the *Christiade* was accompanied by a preface by André de Rivaudeau, who was a Catholic. In this preface, Rivaudeau denounces 'pagan' poetry in terms which suggest Ronsard was among his targets — and also includes a pointed allusion to Bèze: 'Je sai qu'un autre a fait de l'hypocrite et du bigot en la ville que l'on tient pour la plus deplorée de l'Europe' (92). Notwithstanding his opposition to 'paganism', Rivaudeau was an admirer of Ronsard (93). This publication by a Reformer, prefaced by a Catholic who attacks both Ronsard and Bèze, illustrates the fact that in substance there was little if any difference between Reformers and Catholics on this issue.

(ii) Du Bellay's biblical verse

Du Bellay, the author of the highly edifying although allusive *Olive,* had little need to make any concession to the demand for Christian verse. Nonetheless, much of his output in the early 1550s was of biblical inspiration, notably poems in that 1552 collection, the *Autres œuvres de l'invention du translateur,* which contained the attack on Bèze. Notable among them is an *Hymne chrestien* which, echoing the language of the psalms, extols the Creator and identifies a new use for God-given poetical talent:

> O Dieu guerrier! des victoires donneur!
> Donne à mes doigz cete grace et bonheur
> De n'accorder sur ma lyre d'ivoyre
> Pour tout jamais que les vers de ta gloire.
> S'il est ainsi, arriere les vains sons,
> Les vains soupirs et les vaines chansons,
> Arriere amour, et les songes antiques
> Elabourez par les mains poëtiques.
> Ce n'est plus moy, qui vous doy' fredonner:
> Car le Seigneur m'a commandé sonner
> Non l'Odissée, ou la grand' Iliade,
> Mais le discours de l'Israëliade (94).

This poem is followed by a miniature biblical epic, *La mono-machie de David et de Goliath.* There, Du Bellay appeals to God for inspiration, to enable him to extol not a Greek or

Trojan hero, but King David; and he then relates the story of David's victory over Goliath and, in the conclusion, stresses the primacy of biblical over classical poetry:

> Chantez, mes vers, cet immortel honneur,
> Dont vous avez la matiere choizie,
> Ce vous sera plus de gloire et bonheur
> Que les vieux sons d'une fable moizie.
> Car tout au pis, quand vostre poëzie
> Du long oubly devroit estre la proye,
> Si avez vous plus saincte fantaizie
> Que le sonneur des Pergames de Troye (95).

This poem is followed by an ode dedicated to Jean Du Bellay in which the poet extols the Creator for giving man the ability to distinguish between good and evil.

Then comes *La lyre chrestienne,* where Du Bellay begins by again renouncing pagan inspiration:

> Moy cestuy là, qui tant de fois
> Ay chanté la Muse charnelle,
> Maintenant je haulse ma vois
> Pour sonner la Muse eternelle.
> De ceulx là qui n'ont part en elle,
> L'applaudissement je n'attens:
> Jadis ma folie estoit telle,
> Mais toutes choses ont leur temps.
>
> Si les vieux Grecz et les Romains
> Des faux Dieux ont chanté la gloire,
> Seron' nous plus qu'eulx inhumains,
> Taisant du vray Dieu la memoire?
> D'Helicon la fable notoire
> Ne nous enseigne à le vanter:
> De l'onde vive il nous fault boyre,
> Qui seule inspire à bien chanter (96).

He goes on to say that the poetry of the ancients can be used by Christians as models to extol the Creator, and then renounces flattering poetry of the kind that Bèze had deplored:

> O fol, qui chante les honneurs
> De ces faulx Dieux! ou qui s'amuse

> A farder le loz des seigneurs
> Plus aimez qu'amys de la Muse.
> C'est pourquoy la mienne refuse
> De manïer le luc vanteur.
> L'espoir des princes nous abuse,
> Mais nostre Dieu n'est point menteur.

This poem is followed by an equally edifying *Discours sur la louange de la vertu et sur les divers erreurs des hommes*. Here, too, Du Bellay deprecates the wisdom of antiquity, and

> Tant de Dieux, tant de miracles,
> Tant de monstres et d'oracles
> Que nous ont forgez les Grecz (97).

(iii) Ronsard's biblical verse

Ronsard, too, was quickly to make a name for himself as an author of edifying poetry. Ever sensitive to reactions to his verse, he noted that his *Folastries* of 1553, a compilation of Catullan poems, immediately incurred criticism for obscenity (98). These poems were to provide ammunition for those poets (many of them friends of Bèze) who were to write against Ronsard during and after the first civil war. The *Folastries* were to prove an acute and long-term embarrassment to Ronsard, in exactly the same way as the *Poemata* of 1548 were to Bèze. At the time of his death, Ronsard's panegyrists had their work cut out to dispel a reputation for licentiousness, as we shall see.

Immediately after publishing the *Folastries,* Ronsard set about redeeming them by writing edifying verse. The parallel with the situation of Bèze, five years earlier, is again remarkable. The opening lines of his *Hercule chrestien* make clear that this poem, a work of pious syncretism, was conceived as an act of atonement for the *Folastries*:

> Est-il pas temps desormais de chanter
> Un vers chrestien qui puisse contenter,
> Mieux que devant, les chrestiennes oreilles?
> Est-il pas temps de chanter les merveilles

De nostre Dieu? et toute la rondeur
De l'univers emplir de sa grandeur?
Le payen sonne une chanson payenne,
Et le chrestien une chanson chrestienne:
Le vers payen est digne des payens,
Mais le chrestien est digne des chrestiens (99).

That the *Hercule chrestien* was indeed a reparation for the *Folastries* is confirmed by a contemporary (100).

While the *Hercule chrestien* represents a substantial concession to supporters of Christian verse, Ronsard is not forsaking the culture of the ancient pagans in a conversion to explicitly biblical poetry: on the contrary, this poem argues that ancient pagan mythology is a form of divine revelation, for the exploits of Hercules, 'correctly' interpreted, are predictions of events in the life of Christ. Ronsard's syncretist approach marks him out from the Reformers. In pointing to parallels between Hercules and Christ, Ronsard was drawing on a vibrant tradition (101). Most early reactions to his *Hercule chrestien* seem to have been favourable ones (102), but some readers deplored the poem (103).

There is other evidence that Ronsard was sensitive to criticism of his verse and anxious to placate the advocates of edifying poetry. The first sonnet of the *Continuation des Amours,* published in the summer of 1555, seems to refer to the reception accorded to the *Folastries*: 'chacun dit [. . .] que je me dements parlant trop bassement' (104). And the collection *Nouvelle continuation des amours,* published in the second half of 1556, is prefaced by an *Elegie* in which Ronsard, tacitly recognising criticism of the *Folastries,* notes that his readers can pick and choose among his poems, avoiding 'Les vers qui seront folz, amoureux, esventez' (105). And a passage in the epilogue to this *Nouvelle continuation* reflects ruefully on the risk of a hostile reception for this collection of love poems — again, possibly, a reaction to the reception of the *Folastries* (106). Ronsard was to go a long way in the 1550s to meeting the demand for Christian poetry.

The two books of love poems published in 1555 and 1556 are paralleled by two books of *Hymnes* which appeared in those years. Here, too, Ronsard's susceptibility to opinion is evident. He again meets the objections of Christians, but again without abandoning the 'pagan' tradition: he is going halfway (but only halfway) to meet the objections of Reformers like Bèze. Thus, in the *Hymne de la justice* he 'exonerates' the pagan gods by observing that they are simply poetic designations of various aspects of the nature of the one true God (an argument which is older than the Christian faith itself) (107). A passage in the *Hymne de la philosophie* implicitly defends pagan myths by urging that pagan poets' descriptions of the torments of the underworld are in reality representations of the pangs of ambition (108). The tale of the Harpies, likewise, he suggests, is no mere pagan fable, but an edifying warning of the danger of flattery (109). In these examples, Ronsard is showing his readers how to discern edifying moral teaching in the fables of the pagans. He was to develop this idea several times after publishing the *Hymnes*.

(iv) Allegorical poems and biblical poems

Thus, Ronsard and Du Bellay, the objects of Bèze's attack, were themselves authors of edifying verse. True, their views on how theological material may be communicated differed from Bèze's. After his conversion, Bèze seems to have become impatient of any discourse which is not explicitly theological. Du Bellay and Ronsard, on the other hand, convey theological material in a much less direct way. This is well illustrated by Du Bellay's *Olive* which, as we have seen, is on the surface an ordinary love story but which has a deeper meaning as a celebration of the peace between God and man brought about by the Redemption.

Ronsard, too, believed that the function of the poet is a sacred one, and that the most ancient and admirable poets were theologians; and there are elements in the *Odes* which suggest an aspiration to wed the classical tradition to the Christian revelation (110). In general, Reformers seem to have been much more insistent than Catholics that literature should be strictly and literally Christian (111). In embracing the Reformed Church, Bèze turned his back on the syncretist vision characteristic of the Renaissance — and which was perfectly illustrated by the work of Du Bellay and Ronsard.

Besides pointing to veiled edifying meanings to his verse, Ronsard occasionally made the edifying sense explicit, especially in works destined for a popular audience. We find a pronounced biblical tinge in most of the political pamphlets he published at the end of the 1550s. The main theme of the *Exhortation pour la paix,* of September or October 1558, is Christian pacifism. Then, early in 1559, Ronsard wrote *La Paix,* on the same theme: war is the outcome of sin, peace is the fruit of repentance (and is the daughter of God). In the *Discours à Monseigneur le duc de Savoie,* composed in the spring or early summer of 1559, Ronsard discusses the vicissitudes of life and, recalling the example of the author of the psalms, tells how God can make a shepherd into a king and a king into a shepherd; and also uses St. Paul's famous text about the potter to illustrate life's changes (112).

Ronsard and Du Bellay, notwithstanding their low opinion of Marot's psalm translations and their hostility to Bèze, did not want edifying biblical poetry to be seen as the prerogative of their critics; and they sought to forestall any future attacks on their own work on this score.

(v) New attacks by Reformers

But the concessions failed to stem the tide of criticism. One critic was Yves Rouspeau, who later, in 1585, was to publish a versified catechism in an edition of Bèze's *Petit catechisme* (both texts appearing in an edition of the psalms). A preliminary poem in Rouspeau's *De pace et bello carmen elegiacum* (1556) deplores poetry which extols false gods. The poem's title, *Ad priscos et huius temporis poëtas, mendacia scribere solitos* ['To poets, ancient and modern, whose custom is to purvey lies'], sums up its content:

> Scribite vaniloqui mendacia vana poëtæ,
>   Scribite cum fictis somnia ficta diis:
> Nil mihi cum vobis, nos vera referre paramus,
>   Nullus et in nostra carmine fucus erit.
> Non ego Pieridum, nec Phœbi numen adoro,
>   Non ego Parnassi numina montis amo.
> Qui tenebras noctemque meo de pectore pellet,
>   Verus opem nobis Christus Apollo dabit:
> Hunc sitio fontem, procul hinc, procul esto poëtæ
>   Qui miseri latices quærite Aonios.
> Solus hic etenim fons, unde poëta repente
>   Esse queam, sine quo sudor inanis erit (113).

['Compose your empty lies, you lying poets; compose your false nonsense, with your false gods. I shall have nothing to do with you, I am going to relate what is true, and there will be no deceit in my poetry. I do not adore the deity of the daughters of Pierus, or of Phœbus, nor am I in love with the deities of Mount Parnassus. The true Christ, who will drive darkness and the night from my soul, will be my Apollo and will give me help: he is the stream after which I thirst. Be off, be off, you wretched poets who seek the waters of Aonia. For he is the only stream at which I hope to drink and instantly become a poet; without him, all effort will be useless']

In 1560, there appeared an *Hymne à Dieu, pour la delivrance des François de la plus que Egyptienne servitude, en laquelle ils ont esté detenus par le passé*. It contains an *Ode aux poetes françoys*, which reads as follows:

> Divins esprits de la France,
> Vous qui avez accointance
> Au sainct trouppeau des neuf Seurs,
> Vous à qui Phebus addresse
> Une prodigue largesse
> De ses divines doulceurs,
>   Vous, dont la chaste poictrine
> Pleine de fureur divine

Pourroit de hault tonnans vers
Remplir du monde l'enceincte
Chantant la louange saincte
De l'Autheur de l'univers,
    C'est vous qui devriez eslire
Le haut subject que ma lyre
Sonne d'un vulgaire son,
Et d'un industrieux poulce,
Sur harmonie tant doulce
Chanter plus grave chanson.
    C'est vous dont la Muse est digne
Seule d'entonner un hymne
Tel que j'avois entrepris,
Vous les prestres de Parnasse,
Dont le sçavoir et la grace
Sur tous emporte le pris.
    Si l'admirable faconde,
Qui seme parmy le monde
Vostre renom fleurissant,
Si la lyre bien-sonante,
Si la langue bien-disante,
Vient du Seigneur tout-puissant:
    Venez luy en faire hommage,
Venez d'un ardent courage
Et non paresseux ou lent,
De peur qu'il ne redemande
En vain l'usure bien grande
D'un si precieux talent.

The same volume contains an *Ode à Monsieur le Prince de Condé*: this poem is on the same theme, but is couched in less general terms and any reader familiar with the work of Ronsard would have identified its principal target:

Str. 1:

Je ne veux point que mes vers
Soyent flatteusement couvers
Du manteau de voz louanges:
Et moins veux j'avoir le soing
De les envoyer bien loing
Vers les nations estranges.

Pour un fardeau si pesant
Mon dos n'est point suffisant:
Et quand bien la suffisance
Le ciel m'auroit octroyé,
Tel bien seroit employé
A plus utile despence.

Antistro.:

Je laisse tel argument
Pour ceux qui communement
Sont tant curieux de plaire
A ceux qui ont le pouvoir
De guerdonner leur sçavoir
D'un honorable salaire,
Et qui leurs gentils esprits
En l'art des Muses apprins
Veulent employer à dire
Les louanges et honneurs
Des rois et des grans seigneurs
Sur leur flatteresse Lyre.

Epode:

De moy, pour vous contenter,
Et vos oreilles esbatre,
Je ne veus sur mon theatre
Voz louanges presenter,
Ou, contre-suivant la trace
Des flatteurs chanter la race
Portant le nom de Bourbon.
A ceste foys je desire
Dessus les vers de ma lyre
Chanter une autre chanson.

Str. 2:

Car les louanges de Dieu
Obtiendront le premier lieu,
Et marcheront les premieres [. . .] (114)

Like Ronsard, this author adopts the triadic form (strophe, anti-strophe and epode) which is borrowed from Pindar (and which had been derided by Bèze); his opening lines are a direct reply to a passage in Ronsard's celebrated ode dedicated to Michel de L'Hospital (lines 777–782); and the attack on poets who flatter in the hope of reward is also probably directed at Ronsard.

Ronsard was also criticised by one Lavianus for writing love poetry rather than Christian verse. Lavianus's poem does not appear to be extant, nor is anything known about him (so that one cannot say with certainty that he was a Reformer, though this seems more probable than not). His attack on Ronsard is known from a reply to it by Estienne de La Boëtie, *In Lavianum, qui Petrum Ronsardum monuerat ut non amplius amores, sed Dei laudes caneret* ['Against Lavianus, who had warned Peter Ronsard that he should no longer sing of love, but sing the praises of God']:

> Quod Petrum, Laviane, mones ne cantet amores,
>   Utque canat grato iam pius ore Deum,
> Crede mihi, sapis; ille Deo, Laviane, poëta
>   Dignus erit, quisquam si modo dignus erit.
> Ergo agite unanimesque Deum, Laviane, colatis:
>   Te quoque spes aliqua est posse placere Deo.
> Scilicet ille colet divino numina cantu;
>   Nec tu forte minus, si, Laviane, taces (115).

['You warn Peter that he should not sing of love, Lavianus, and that with thankful lips he should dutifully extol the Creator. It would be sensible of you to believe me when I say that that poet will be worthy of God if anyone is. Therefore both you and he can worship the Creator — for there is some hope that you too may be able to be pleasing to God. He, obviously, will worship the deity with his divine peotry; and you can worship God no less well, Lavianus, by keeping your mouth shut']

(vi) Bèze's letter to Volmar

In 1560, Bèze published a letter which interests us, and which was to be reprinted several times thereafter. Addressed to his old preceptor and mentor Melchior Volmar, the letter was published in Geneva with Bèze's *Confessio christianæ fidei et ejusdem collatio cum papisticis hæresibus*. Bèze explains at the outset that he wishes to accompany this profession of his faith with an account of his earlier life, before his conversion. It emerges from this letter that while he was still a pupil of Volmar at Orléans in the late 1520s and at Bourges in the early 1530s (thus, long before he made the acquaintance of Peletier and Ronsard), Bèze had been guided towards the views of the Reformers by his preceptor: 'But by far the greatest of the benefits I received from you, is that you so completely imbued me with a knowledge of true piety, drawn from the purest stream (as it were) of the word of God, that if I did not revere you and respect you not just as a teacher but as a father I would be the most ungrateful and inhuman of men'.

Bèze then explains how, from 1535, he studied law at Orléans; but his heart was in the humanities and he spent much more time in reading Greek and Latin than on his legal studies. 'I took a wonderful delight in the study of poetry, to which I felt drawn by some innate force; as a result, I became very close to all the most learned members of that university, people who all now enjoy great esteem in France, and by their example they impelled me to ally the study of literature to the study of law, and they impelled me also to amuse myself in writing poetry. Here, then, before I was twenty years of age, I wrote almost all those poems which I published some years later and dedicated to you'. Bèze is referring here, as his editors observe, to the literary circle which formed around the illustrious humanist Jean de Dampierre.

Bèze then broaches the delicate issue of the content of some of these poems, and in words which seem to imply that his enemies were already reading his poetry as though it were biographical: 'Even if some of those poems are somewhat licentious, for they were written in imitation of Catullus and Ovid, nonetheless I had little fear at the time and have little fear now that people who then knew me as I was would judge my way of life on the basis of those fictitious amusements'. We see here a further clear parallel between the *fortuna* of Bèze and that of Ronsard: as Bèze's life was pilloried by Catholic commentators on the basis of a literal reading of his *Poemata*, Ronsard was to be accused of all sorts of misdemeanours by Reformers on the strength of his poetry, notably the *Folastries*.

Bèze then describes how he was given ecclesiastical benefices he had not asked for, and had the expectation of further benefices; and how he was torn between following those dictates of conscience which the early acquaintance of Volmar had prompted in him, and enjoying the blandishments which Satan put before him — friendships, leisure, and wealth; and there were others — the allurement of pleasures; the charm of fame, which came especially with the publication of his poetry; and the expectation of advancement at court. But it was the will of God that Bèze, who had knowingly set out on this perilous worldly path, should escape the perils. He overcame the allurement of illicit vice by marrying, albeit at first secretly and with a promise to confirm the marriage openly in the Church of God as soon as possible; and 'the most merciful Father had me also reject firmly that fame and that offer of advancement, not just to the amazement of my friends but also with many of them reproaching me, and describing me in jest as a "new philosopher"'. But the break with the past was still not definitive; he was still torn between on the one hand his conscience and his wife who wanted the marriage openly solemnised (which would require resignation of his benefices), and on the other the blandishments of Satan and the promise of further benefices on the death of his brother.

God took pity on him, afflicting him with a near-mortal disease; so that, faced with the imminent prospect of divine judgement, he repented, and renewed his promise to embrace the true religion. 'At one and the same time, therefore, it was possible to leave my sick bed and to break all bonds; having put together a little pack of my belongings, I abandoned my country, my family and my friends, and followed Christ, and withdrew in voluntary exile with my wife to Geneva'. He adds that a little later he secured a post in Greek at Lausanne, before becoming a pastor in Geneva. He concludes by offering the work to Volmar as being better and holier than those epigrams he once asked Bèze to publish. 'As for them, who was the first to condemn them if it was not I, their wretched author? And who detests them more cordially than I do today? Would that they could at last be buried in perpetual oblivion; and, since what is done cannot be undone, may God grant my wish that those who now read writings of mine which are entirely diverse from those, should prefer to congratulate me for the favours God has wrought in me, rather than to accuse a man who is willingly confessing and deploring the sin of his youth' (116).

CHAPTER IV

Reconciliation?

(i) Du Bellay, Ronsard and the 'moyenneurs'

The concessions which Ronsard and Du Bellay made to the demand for Christian poetry reflect their interest in, and openness to, comments made about their work. But a willingness to adopt an accommodating stance towards their critics, many of them Reformers, may also be the reflection of a conciliatory attitude towards the Reformation itself: we saw that both Ronsard and Du Bellay were appalled by the corruption which the Reformers reacted against. Moreover, both Ronsard and Du Bellay, as poets, had a role, which became increasingly important, as political and social commentators: they observed the increasingly severe civil strife which followed in the wake of religious division, and were profoundly concerned by it. This fact, too, may have inclined them towards a conciliatory stance on the question of the proper subject of poetry.

For both Ronsard and Du Bellay seem to have sympathised with the 'moyenneurs', advocates of the middle way, who sought to remove corruption in the Church and to arrive at doctrinal unity through scholarly enquiry and mutual concession. Du Bellay, a member of a notably conciliatory family, was, as well as being an implacable foe of corruption in the Church, an advocate of freedom of expression (and was himself threatened with the Inquisition for having written *Les*

Regrets (117)). It seems safe to conclude that he was committed by temperament to the middle way. However, his death on 1 January 1560 largely takes him out of our story (though, as we shall see, long after the death of Du Bellay, Bèze was to return to the attack against him).

The evidence for Ronsard's sympathy with the 'moyenneurs' is overwhelming. We have seen him attack the obscurantism of the Sorbonne and the 'fraudes rommaines'. He expressed admiration for some of the most prominent advocates of the 'middle way' — Michel de L'Hospital, Paul de Foix and Jean de Monluc (118). In the *Elegie à Guillaume Des Autels* of 1560, he urged conciliation (119). In 1562 and 1563, each of his major attacks on the Reformers blames corruption in the Church for the schism (120). He commented dispassionately on individual Reformers even at the height of civil war (121), and deprecated extremist zeal (122). He distinguished, as 'moyenneurs' all did, between religious opinion and subversion, attacking only 'le Huguenot mutin, l'heretique meschant' (123). Towards the end of his life, unsurprisingly, he expressed support for Henry of Navarre as heir to the throne (124). Ronsard's evident openness to an accommodation with the Reformers at this time was to lead to interesting developments.

(ii)   The role of Louis Des Masures

At the end of the 1550s, a *rapprochement* between Ronsard and the Reformers seems to have been attempted. The central figure is a mutual friend of Ronsard and Bèze from very early days: Louis Des Masures — who, incidentally, was another associate of Peletier (125). As secretary of Cardinal Jean de Lorraine, Des Masures had spent many years at the court of Francis I, where he knew the leading writers of the time. He was banished from France for reasons which are unknown, but which may have been related to his religious views (126). Jean de Lorraine expected to secure his rehabilitation, but died as the two of them were returning to France from the papal conclave of 1549. In the course of that latter journey, the Cardinal sent Des Masures on a mission to Geneva, and it was in the course of that mission that he met Bèze; whether or not Des Masures had an interest in the Reformation before, he certainly did from then on.

Des Masures's meeting with Bèze took place in Lausanne early in 1550 (127); and Bèze, in a letter of 19 April 1550 to Calvin, commends Des Masures's intellectual ability, his likely conversion to the Reformation and his translations of some of the psalms; subject to Calvin's approval, Bèze proposes to share the task of translating the psalms with this man (128). Later, in 1554, in a letter to Farel, Bèze noted that Des Masures was seriously ill and that he, Bèze, was inviting him to reflect again about the possibility of adopting the Reformed faith (129). A few years later, Bèze was to extol Des Masures's *De Babylonis ruina* (130).

Des Masures, for his part, acknowledged his indebtedness to Bèze. In a recently-discovered letter of 9 February 1564, he noted that he had been urged by his friends 'and by the frequent letters of Bèze and Spifame' to adopt the Reformed faith (131). In a poem published that year, he lengthily described his debt to Bèze (after God) for his adoption of the Reformed faith (132). A few years later, in a poem in Bèze's *Poemata* in 1569, Des Masures declared that he had been led to religious truth by Bèze himself (133). There is abundant evidence of Des Masures's discipleship of Bèze in the second edition of his *Poemata,* of 1574 (134); and he published a French translation of Bèze's *Summa doctrinæ de re sacramentaria* (135).

Unsurprisingly, Des Masures was an eloquent advocate of Christian verse: in 1557, he publicly renounced 'pagan' poetry such as the *Aeneid* (he had previously published a translation of this work, which had been praised by many, including Du Bellay) (136). In the same year, he published his translations of twenty psalms. In an interesting prefatory poem in this work, Des Masures declared, as Marot had done, that he would not look to the pagan gods for inspiration; and the poem recalls the irony of Old Testament prophets about people who make 'gods' with their own hands and who then fear and worship what they themselves have made. Des Masures adds that the stream of Pegasus provides inspiration only for fables, lies and carnal love, but the inspiration of the holy Spirit fills souls with divine love, and it was this Spirit which dictated the psalms to King David and which has prompted Des Masures to translate them (137). Later, in his trilogy of plays about King David, first published in Geneva in 1563, Des Masures again stressed the need for edifying and 'true' poetry, as distinct from the unedifying fables of the pagans (138). Clearly, after translating the *Aeneid,* Des Masures moved to a conception of the role of the poet identical to that of Bèze.

At what stage did Des Masures adopt the Reformed faith? As we have seen, his banishment from France may have been linked with his religious views; and at all events his definitive conversion was influenced by his encounter with Bèze in 1550. His change of religion seems to have been quietly maturing during the 1550s: he was later to confess that he had been held back by fear and an attachment to worldly goods (139). It has been argued that the selection of psalms he published in translation in 1557 reveals his agonised hesitation about a change of religion (140). In 1558, the serious illness of his four-year-old son Claude prompted him to 'abandon Satan' and 'follow Christ' (141). He then founded a small Reformed church in Saint-Nicolas-du-Port, near Nancy (142). In January 1562, a public baptism performed in Saint-Nicolas by a pastor from Metz led to an armed force being sent to arrest Des Masures, who fled to Metz; the execution of a humble Reformer as a scapegoat clinched his commitment to the Reformed faith (143).

At some time in the 1550s, Des Masures had written a long autobiographical poem detailing the vicissitudes of Fortune to which he had been subject. The poem tells of his links with poets and patrons at the court of Francis I, of his exile, of Jean de Lorraine's hope of rehabilitating him, and of the frustration of that hope when his patron died on the journey from Italy to France (in May 1550) — which led Des Masures to resume his life of exile; he has now found employment in Lorraine. There is no trace of Calvinist sentiment in this poem. On the contrary:

Des Masures describes the students of a Catholic theological college as 'La jeunesse vouée à Dieu et à son temple' (l. 112), he repeatedly extols Cardinal Jean de Lorraine, and dispassionately evokes the papal election of 1549–50 (l. 355–358).

Very interestingly, Des Masures chose to dedicate this poem to Ronsard. The poem is a rejection of all that Bèze and his followers were saying about Ronsard: it notes Ronsard's pre-eminence as a poet, extols his love poetry and, in an accompanying Latin poem *Ad P. Ronsardum et Ioac. Bellaium, Poëtas,* praises Ronsard's emulation of Pindar ('Te magnum, Ronsarde, refers [. . .] Pindaron' — Bèze had derided Ronsard's resurrection of the Pindaric ode). Equally significantly, Ronsard published Des Masures's *Discours* in his own *Second livre des meslanges,* of 1559; with the poem, he included Des Masures's Latin poem and two sonnets which Des Masures had written in praise of him, Ronsard (144). Also in 1559, Des Masures published a *Chant pastoral* on the return to Lorraine of the Duke, with his wife Claude de France: this work is closely modelled on Ronsard's own *Chant pastoral* on the marriage of this couple, and contains a glowing tribute to Ronsard (145).

It seems clear that by 1559, Des Masures was committed to the Reformed faith, though the fact may not have been widely known. It has been suggested that the autobiographical poem and the Latin poem which accompanied it were inspired by Bèze who sought, through Des Masures, to win Ronsard over to the Reformation (146). Certainly, Des Masures's praise of Ronsard as a Pindaric poet could be seen as an interesting 'atonement' for Bèze's derision of Ronsard's discipleship of the Greek poet. But, given the non-sectarian nature of Des Masures's poems, it is perhaps more likely that they betoken a desire on the part of Des Masures, perhaps still wavering in religion himself, to have done with aesthetic and theological partialities.

(iii) Ronsard's reaction to Des Masures's overtures

Whatever the reason for Des Masures's overtures, Ronsard was receptive to them. In the *Second livre des meslanges,* he followed Des Masures's poems with a sonnet of his own addressed to him, deploring his departure from France and the departures of Peletier and Bèze:

> Masures, tu m'as veu, bien que la France à l'heure
> Encor ne m'enroloit entre les bons esprits,
> Et sans barbe et barbu j'ay releu tes escrits,
> Qui engardent qu'Enée en la France ne meure.
>
> Ah, que je suis marry, qu'encore ne demeure
> En France ce troupeau divinement apris,
> Qui sous le Roy François pour emporter le prix
> Chantoit à qui mieux mieux d'une Muse meilleure!
>
> Pour une opinion de Baize est delogé,
> Tu as par faux raport durement voyagé,
> Et Peletier le docte a vagué comme Ulysse:
>
> Phœbus, tu ne vaux rien, et vous ne valez rien,
> Muses, jouët à foux: puisqu'en vostre service
> Vos servans n'ont receu que du mal pour du bien (147).

It is distinctly possible that Ronsard hoped to re-establish good relations with Bèze. It is worth recalling that the collection in which this sonnet appeared was published shortly after the death of Henry II, whose hostility to the Reformation was implacable, and Ronsard may have felt that the prospects for conciliation had improved with the death of the king (148). The hypothesis that Ronsard sought reconciliation with Bèze is confirmed by comments of Des Masures which we shall shortly look at. Ronsard does not endorse the Reformed faith (on the contrary, he notes that Bèze has left 'pour une opinion', and opinion meant heresy), but it was probably brave of him to refer so positively in 1559 to Bèze, Peletier and Des Masures, three poets and erstwhile friends who all had (at the least) links with the Reformation.

Ronsard almost certainly sent this sonnet to Des Masures, and with a sequel which is interesting enough to justify a momentary digression. An eminent young German poet, Paul

Schede, who is better known by his humanist name of Melissus, made the acquaintance of Des Masures while the latter was in exile in Lorraine or in Germany. Their respective work shows that the acquaintance between them was a close one. Des Masures, it seems, helped give Melissus a knowledge of Ronsard — and a very high opinion of him. Moreover, Melissus was to publish a Latin translation of the sonnet by Ronsard we have just read. Melissus's admiration for Ronsard is all the more interesting as he seems to have been a thoroughly committed Reformer — he lived in Geneva from 1568 to 1571, and knew Bèze, and was praised by Bèze. Indeed, he was an admirer of Bèze's psalm translation — and an emulator of it: he translated the psalms into German, with the objective, as he put it, of doing for German what Bèze and Marot had done for French (149).

(iv)   Ronsard's first collected edition (1560)

In 1560, the simmering religious disputes first exploded into substantial strife, notably with the Conspiracy of Amboise of March. In that year, the first collected edition of Ronsard's work appeared (the *privilegium* is dated 20 September). The volume of *Œuvres* reflects the fraught situation, notably in an elegy dedicated to Guillaume Des Autels which stresses the need for Catholics to publish books in defence of their faith and which deplores the Amboise plot (150). And it reflects intimately Ronsard's attitude towards Louis Des Masures, whom he must by now have known had become a Reformer.

In this edition, Ronsard dedicated to Des Masures the *Hymne de la mort,* which he had previously dedicated to Pierre Paschal. He also dedicated to Des Masures the fifth book of his *Poëmes.* One of the new works in that fifth book is an elegy addressed to Des Masures himself. At the outset, Ronsard notes that his own work is made up of a great variety of poems, like a highly diverse landscape which an observer will find partly attractive, partly unattractive. Or, it is like a banquet which a king lays out for his guests, containing dishes which will appeal to some tastes but not to others: those who read his books are like guests at his feast — and those who complain that some of his dishes are not to their taste are not obliged to partake of his feast. He makes it clear who he is referring to:

> Je m'estonne de ceulx de la nouvelle foy
> Qui pour me hault louer disent tousjours de moy,
> Sy Ronsard ne cachoit son talent dedans terre,
> Or parlant de l'amour, or parlant de la guerre,
> Et qu'il voulust du tout chanter de Jesuchrist,
> Il seroit tout parfaict, car il a bon esprit,
> Mais Sathan l'a seduict, le pere des mensonges,
> Qui ne luy fait chanter que fables et que songes.
> O pauvres abusez, que le cuider sçavoir
> Plus que toute l'Eglise, a laissé decevoir!
> Tenez vous en vos peaux et ne jugez personne.
> Je suis ce que je suis, ma conscience est bonne,
> Et Dieu, à qui le cœur des hommes apparoist,
> Sonde ma volunté et seul il la connoist (151).

Interestingly, Ronsard affects to believe that his critics are all Reformers. This was far from being the case; but it suggests that from the earliest days, Ronsard may have followed the censures directed at his poetry by Bèze with particular interest. Equally interesting is the fact that while his rejoinder to his critics is vigorous, it is also moderate: the 'banquet' topos dilutes the invective, suggesting his critics are simply ill-mannered guests.

The volume of *Œuvres* of 1560 reveals Ronsard's attitude towards another poet who had joined the Reformers. It contains an elegy addressed to Robert de La Haye, an associate of Bèze (his adherence to the Reformed faith was about to become public). Links between Ronsard and La Haye seem to have been fairly close, and they were of long standing. In 1551, La Haye had written a poem in praise of Ronsard and Du Bellay, titled *De I. Bellaio et P. Ronsardo,* which was published the following year in Du Bellay's *Quatriesme livre de l'Eneide*; Du Bellay and Ronsard had both published poems in praise of him that year (152). It seems that La Haye reproached Ronsard for the obscenity of the *Livret de Folastries* of 1553 (153). The 1555 edition of Ronsard's *Odes* contains a poem by La Haye, titled *Henrico Regi Robertus Hayus de P. Ronsardo,* which extolls Ronsard's projected *Franciade*; Ronsard was to paraphrase La Haye's poem in his own *Elegie à Pierre L'Escot* of 1560 (154).

The *Elegie à Robert de La Haye* is one of the most beautiful new poems in the 1560 collected edition of Ronsard. There, reflections on the world's vanity (inspired by the book of *Ecclesiastes*) are followed by comment on La Haye's happy influence on the poet:

> Lors de mes passions, desquelles je me deuls,
> Tu gouvernes la bride, et je vois où tu veulx [. . .]
> Puis me parlant de Dieu tu m'enleves l'esprit
> A cognoistre par foy que c'est que Jesuchrist,
> Et comme par sa mort de la mort nous delivre,
> Et par son sang nous faict eternellement vivre.
> En ce poinct, de ta voix plus douce que le miel
> Tu me ravis du corps et m'emportes au ciel,
> Tu romps mes passions, et seul me fais cognoistre
> Que rien plus sainct que l'homme au monde ne peut
> naistre (155).

This passage is eloquent testimony to Ronsard's conciliatory religious sentiment: it shows him taking instruction in theology from a Reformer, and recording the fruit of that instruction in highly edifying verse.

(v)   The Marot-Bèze psalms

Meanwhile, the Reformers' psalm translations were still a point of contention between Reformers and Ronsard. When, in 1561, the government permitted publication of the Marot-Bèze translation, Florent Chrestien saluted the decision — and with pointed remarks about 'profane' poets, by which (as his title indicates) he especially meant Ronsard. The poem, which has recently been discovered, is titled *Ad Poetas profanos et maxime Ronsardum* ['To profane poets and especially Ronsard']. It recalls that ancient legislators wisely kept poets at arm's length from society, since few poets ever sought true virtue, and most of them were gluttonous and slothful; now, however, Charles IX is bringing back a golden age, in which vain poets who give to false gods the honour due to the true God are invited to listen to the message of the supreme being (156).

Bèze, for his part, returned to the charge in favour of biblical poetry in January 1562. The following passage, written around that time, picks up the theme in *Abraham* with which we began. It is found in a poem published in Pierre de Courcelles's *Le Cantique des cantiques de Salomon, mis en vers françois* of 1564, and may also have appeared earlier:

> L'homme chrestien des Muses allaité,
> Favorisé du ciel et de nature,
> Ne doit ailleurs qu'en la saincte Escriture
> Avoir l'esprit rendu et arresté.
> Maints aujourd'huy, confits en vanité,
> Ne chantent rien qu'une Venus impure,
> Et de choisir autre subject n'ont cure
> Plus profitable à la posterité.
>
> L'un se complaint des rigueurs de sa dame,
> Pensant ainsi fleschir son rude cueur:
> L'autre au rebours se vante du bonheur
> Qu'il a receu en l'amoureuse flâme.
> Esgal ennuy sollicite leur ame:
> Car cil qui ha tant de bien et faveur,
> De jalousie esprouve la fureur,
> Et de douleur, comme l'autre, se pasme.
>
> Mais toy qui es poëte bien appris,
> Cognoissant bien les poetiques esprits
> Estre subjects aux flammes amoureuses:
> Pour eviter les traicts de Cupidon,
> As arresté ton lyrique fredon
> Sur les amours celestes et heureuses.
>
> Or pleust à Dieu que tous ces amoureux,
> Qui sont ainsi palles et langoureux,
> Fussent espris d'affections pareilles:
> Tant de propos corrompus et mauvais,

> Et de chansons impudiques, jamais
> N'offenseroyent les chrestiennes oreilles (157).

Courcelles includes in this compilation his own poem attacking profane erotic verse:

> Chassez doncques ces chansons,
> Amis, folles et lubriques,
> Et chantez en plaisans sons
> Ce Cantique des Cantiques,
> Qui ne parle que de Christ,
> De Christ et de son Eglise (158).

(vi) Ronsard attacks Reformers' psalm translations

Ronsard was to attack the Reformers' psalm translations in one of the poems which were to form the *Discours des miseres.* The poem, the *Responce aux injures,* issued in pamphlet form in 1563, was an immediate best-seller (159). In this poem (lines 1011–42), Ronsard claims that he has single-handedly brought the poetic inspiration of ancient Rome and Greece to France — and had not realized that the Reformers were to make of poetry the 'apast de la bouche heretique / Pour servir de chansons aux valets de boutique'. The heretics' 'chansons' for the popular classes are very probably the psalm translations which were set to music, and massively disseminated after permission to publish had been accorded in 1561. Ronsard evidently held the same view of the Reformers' liturgy (as of so many other things) as Montaigne who, alluding to the Reformers, deplored '[. . .] l'usage promiscue, temeraire et indiscret des sainctes et divines chansons que le Sainct Esprit a dicté en David' (*Des prieres: Essais,* I, lvi).

CHAPTER V

'Ce guerrier de Baize'

(i) Bèze and an 'Evangile armée'

As the religious division led to armed insurrection and civil war, Ronsard followed events with keen interest: indeed, he seems to have become the most influential French political commentator (and defender of the Catholic faith) (160). In 1560, as we have seen, he deplored the Conspiracy of Amboise, though without naming Bèze (who was suspected of having had a hand in it (161)). And in 1561, as we know from his *Responce aux injures,* he was present at the Colloquy of Poissy, where Bèze led the contingent of Reformed theologians (162). Ronsard's reaction to Poissy seems to have been confined to helping to write a facetious poem purportedly presenting the views of each of the assembled theologians on love — and which, in the case of Bèze, implicitly calls to mind the erotic poems he had disowned (163).

In 1562, as strife degenerated into outright civil war, Ronsard adopted a role akin to that of a present-day journalist. For him, poetry is no longer the preserve of a community of scholar-poets: it is a mass medium — and a medium which Ronsard is deploying with persuasive intent at a moment of national crisis. His references to Bèze reflect that fact: he is no longer content with elegant allusion to an unnamed target. The name of Bèze becomes a refrain, and a byword for sedition.

Ronsard went to watch Bèze preach (164) — and observed that beneath his cloak, Bèze wore a sword. Ronsard's ironies about this ('Quelle Evangille helas! Quel charitable zele!') seem to have reflected a widely-held view (165). Antoine de Bourbon complained to Bèze about Reformers attending religious services with weapons — to which Bèze's rejoinder was that 'les armes entre les mains des sages portent la paix' (166).

In April, May and June 1562, Bèze recruited soldiers for the armies of the Reformers; and, in the autumn of 1562, after the Reformers ceded ports in Normandy to the English, Ronsard singled out Bèze for particularly eloquent denunciation. A justly famous passage in the *Continuation du Discours à la Royne* accuses Bèze of filling France with soldiers resembling the Theban warriors which sprang from the dragon's teeth, of inflicting on the nation the barbarity of the Goths, Tartars and Scythians, of preaching an *Evangile armée,* of introducing a *Christ empistollé tout noircy de fumée* and of leading France headlong into sedition. In their replies to Ronsard, Reformers sought to exonerate Bèze of warmongering (167).

In the midst of propaganda on affairs of state, Ronsard does not overlook Bèze's role as an author of erotic poetry. He is perhaps mindful of that preface to *Abraham* in which Bèze had attacked love poetry as well as his, Ronsard's, odes. Whereas Bèze had told the Pléiade to turn from love poetry to theology, Ronsard now urges the Reformer to make the opposite switch, and 'hold the reins of the swans of Paphos' (i.e. write love poetry, for the swan is an emblem of Venus, who was adored at Paphos), rather than attack the Church and plunge France into war (168). It is no doubt a discreet reminder of the fact that the Reformer, prior to his conversion, had been a celebrated author of love poems. This attack on Bèze — like just about everything Ronsard wrote in these poems — evoked several eloquent replies by Reformers (169).

The most caustic passage in Ronsard's whole polemic with the Reformers, in the *Remonstrance au peuple,* contains a derisive list of unnamed Reformers. Bèze is referred to as:

> Un mocqueur, un pipeur, un bon nieur de debte,
> Qui vend un benefice et à deux et à trois,
> Un paillard, un causeur, un renyé françoys.

The allusion to the same benefice sold more than once identifies Bèze, who was charged by other contemporaries with an act of dishonesty of this kind (170).

The same poem contains an apparent rejoinder to Bèze's remark about flattering poets who convert the devil into an angel:

> Voyant cette escriture ils diront en courroux
> Et quoy, ce gentil sot escrit doncq contre nous!
> Il flatte les seigneurs, il fait d'un diable un ange (171).

Ronsard is almost certainly echoing, and rebutting, the passage cited above from the 1551 edition of Bèze's translation of the psalms.

In the *Response aux injures* of 1563, Ronsard attempts to provoke Bèze to enter the arena and write against him. He refers to him as 'ce grand guerrier et grand soldat de Baize', an allusion to the Reformer's supposed 'warmongering' in 1562, and refers to him later in the same poem as an 'Orion armé' (the constellation Orion was depicted in books of astronomy as an armed warrior). Ronsard targetted several other passages in these poems at Bèze (172).

The civil war, and the polemical exchange which accompanied it, widened the division between Ronsard and Bèze into a gulf. Ronsard's most telling passage against the Reformation is probably the one deploring the 'Evangile armée' — of Bèze, precisely. This passage was frequently imitated by other propagandists, a fact which will have done nothing to endear Ronsard to Bèze (173).

(ii) Bèze's friends strike back: Florent Chrestien

Bèze did not, so far as is known, respond to Ronsard's attacks immediately (174), though he was to do so a few years later. Meantime, Bèze's friends (who had also been friends of

Ronsard) took up the cudgels on his behalf. Florent Chrestien was one of those friends (175). Ronsard's attitude towards Chrestien had been (according to the poet himself) a favourable one: '[je] l'avois aymé, festié et chery' (176); and Chrestien confirms that they were acquaintances (177). But in 1561, as we have seen, Chrestien had deprecated pagan poetry and commended the psalms in a poem addressed to 'profane poets, and especially Ronsard'. Now, with the outbreak of war and Ronsard's overt defence of the Catholic faith, Chrestien became an out-and-out foe of Ronsard. In 1563 he published a *Seconde responce de F. de la Baronie à Messire Pierre de Ronsard Prestre-Gentilhomme Vandomois, Evesque futur,* accusing him of (*inter alia*) vanity, avarice, gluttony, sedition, atheism and pederasty; Bèze (says Chrestien) will not deign to reply to Ronsard's provocations (178).

In 1564, Chrestien returned to the fray with an *Apologie ou Deffense d'un homme chrestien pour imposer silence aus sottes reprehensions de M. Pierre Ronsard, soy disant non seulement Poëte, mais aussi maistre des Poëtastres.* In this pamphlet, a reply to the prose *Epistre* which prefaces Ronsard's *Recueil des nouvelles poësies,* Chrestien adds to his earlier charges against Ronsard, accusing him of perfidy, plagiarism and drunkenness (179). It is possible that Chrestien also had a hand in the writing of one of the most scurrilous of the pamphlets against Ronsard, *Le temple de Ronsard où la legende de sa vie est briefvement descrite* (along with Jacques Grévin, who certainly had a hand in it) (180). Although these works were published anonymously, it seems that Ronsard knew Chrestien had written against him (181). Chrestien was to return to the charge in 1567 (in *Deux hymnes genethliaques,* on the baptism of Condé's son) attacking 'la profane Muse / De ces Poetes lascifs' and commending 'la saincte Poësie / Dont l'ame de David jadis estoit saisie' (182).

(iii)   Bèze's friends: Louis Des Masures

Still more significantly, Louis Des Masures was also almost certainly among those Reformed poets who denounced Ronsard. He is the probable author of a *Replique sur la response faite par Messire Pierre Ronsard [. . .]*, 'par D.M. Lescaldin', of 1563 (183). At the outset, the author observes that Ronsard has tried to provoke Bèze to write against him, but Bèze has better things to do than crush Ronsard; accordingly, he, the author, is carrying out the task on behalf of Bèze. This verse pamphlet, which is a point-by-point rebuttal of Ronsard's *Responce aux injures,* reflects the gulf which the war has created between erstwhile friends: Ronsard is here castigated as 'mesdisant, inepte, et plein de gloire, / Athée, ambitieux, detracteur faux et vain' (l. 8 – 9), as 'yvre, orgueilleux, fier et sot' (l. 398), as 'Athée, ambitieux, verolé, sot et prestre' (l. 484) and as 'Athée, enragé, diable, sourd, phrenetique' (l. 1240).

Interestingly, this *Replique* contains what is probably an echo of conversations Ronsard had had with one of his Reformed friends, possibly Des Masures himself, shortly before the outbreak of the war. The passage I am about to cite (lines 771 – 780 of the *Replique*) replies to Ronsard's statement in his *Responce aux injures* that he abhorred corruption in the Church but would never leave it (l. 449 – 454):

> Ainsi en ce qui suit monstres-tu que tu songes,
> Et qu'à tort et travers tu jettes tes mensonges,
> Quand tu dis des abus te vouloir separer
> Mais que tu veux pourtant mille morts endurer
> Ains que l'Eglise ailleurs puisse voir te retraire.
> O menteur impudent! Qu'as-tu dit au contraire
> Toy-mesmes à quelcun, ensemble devisans
> A Sainct Germain en Laye, il n'y a pas deux ans?
> Or tu t'es ravisé: l'Eglise tu embrasses,
> De l'Eglise à jamais tu veux suivre les traces.

It is possible that this is an attempt to discredit Ronsard in the eyes of those of his own faith by depicting him as vacillating; but this passage dovetails perfectly with the surmise that immediately before the war Ronsard's attitude towards the Reformers had been a very conciliatory one, and that like so many Catholic intellectuals in the months prior to the war, he was a 'moyenneur'.

The polemical *Replique* is not the only place in which Des Masures attacked Ronsard after the outbreak of war. In a preliminary poem in *Babylone, ou la ruine de la grande cité, et du regne tyrannique de la grande paillarde babylonienne,* he published another attack:

> Les autres chanteront en vaine poësie
> Les dieux forgez par eux, et à leur phantasie,
> Diront les faits des rois vaillans, nobles et preux,
> Fortunes, guerres, paix, songes de cerveaux creux
> Forgez en leur Parnasse à la crouppe jumelle,
> Ou au cerveau cornu de la lune et, comme elle
> Inconstans et legers. Moy, d'un cœur magnanime,
> Si ton esprit, Seigneur, me conforte et anime
> (Seul esprit veritable), en ta verité pure
> Ta louange diray, qui eternelle dure.
> Je veux ton nom, Seigneur, exalter desormais,
> Seul nom digne de gloire et d'honneur à jamais.

Though Ronsard is not named, he must be Des Masures's principal target (184). This work appeared in 1563, with a Latin translation in 1569.

Then, in 1564, in the poem in praise of Bèze published in his *Vingtsix Cantiques,* Des Masures again alluded to his former friends on the other side of the religious divide:

> [. . .] Que pleust à Dieu que ceux qui s'arrestent encor
> En la fange, laquelle à eux plus chere qu'or
> Les retient enfonsés, eussent receu la grace
> D'en sortir, et entrer en ceste heureuse trace;
> Que l'estude conforme entre eux et nous amis
> Qui nous joignit ensemble, et qui tant les a mis
> A poursuivre le train que joye en malheur donne,
> Fust encor à nous jointe en ceste cause bonne;
> Qu'aux vers chastes et saints fust leur gloire, et en lieu
> Du monde à Dieu contraire, ils chantassent de Dieu:
> Qu'ils chantassent de Dieu en pseaumes et cantiques

La puissance, les faicts, les bontés authentiques;
Que leurs celestes dons fussent au seul honneur
Employés de celui qui en est le donneur;
Que ceux qui ont de Dieu receu ces graces belles
Entendissent au vray qu'ayans abusé d'elles
A toute vanité, le Seigneur est là haut
Auquel se presenter et conte rendre faut;
Que de lui, qui tout voit, il convient, sans contendre,
Salaire du mespris et de l'abus attendre,
Et que leurs vers, au jour triste et malencontreux,
Seront tesmoins produits en jugement contre eux.
Or Dieu de qui la voix à leur oreille crie,
Leur veuille ouvrir les yeux, humblement je l'en prie.

Des Masures was clearly anguished by the widening division (185).

(iv)   Bèze's friends: Robert de La Haye

The war separated Ronsard from another poet now committed to the Reformation. Robert de La Haye had been praised by Ronsard in 1560, but in September 1562 had negotiated, on behalf of Condé, the treaty which led to an English army invading Normandy — to the outrage of (among many others) Ronsard, who deplored the deal in the *Continuation du discours à la royne.* Hardly surprisingly, successive editions of Ronsard's complete works reflect a new attitude towards La Haye. In the 1567 edition, Ronsard cut many lines of praise from the end of the *Elegie à Robert de La Haye.* In the 1571 edition, he removed La Haye's Latin poem in praise of the *Franciade,* which had featured in earlier editions. In 1578, he suppressed the mention of La Haye in the title of the elegy he had dedicated to him in 1560.

(v)   Bèze's friends: Antoine de La Roche-Chandieu

Antoine de La Roche-Chandieu, another foe of Ronsard, was also an associate of Bèze (186). Chandieu, who signed himself 'Zamariel' (which means 'champ de Dieu' in Hebrew), wrote the first of three works in a collection titled *Response aux calomnies contenues au Discours et Suyte du Discours sur les miseres de ce temps*: Chandieu exhorts pious poets to use their poetic gifts to rebut Ronsard, and attacks Ronsard for his subservience to monarchs, for failing to realize that custom does not make a religion true, and for being essentially an atheist; he presents an allegorical figure, 'Theologie' (the answer to the 'Opinion' of Ronsard's *Discours à la Royne*) who relates that she has been attacked by the 'fureur poëtique' of Epicurean poets, but supported by the verse of King David; Chandieu extols the Conspiracy of Amboise; and he describes Ronsard's supposed fall from poet to priest (187).

The confrontation between Ronsard and Reformers in the civil war of 1562–63 was, in a sense, simply the continuation of an existing debate of which Bèze's preface to *Abraham* is the first certain manifestation, and which had rumbled on for more than a decade. As the social consequences of religious division became evident in the late 1550s, conciliatory spirits drew back from the abyss and sought conciliation. But then the seismic shock of war widened the division to a chasm.

(vi)   The sonnet on the perfection of Bèze

In 1564, with the war over, Ronsard published his *Recueil des nouvelles Poësies*. The collection, in three books, contains poems which, he says in an introductory *Epistre,* are 'toutes diferentes de stille et d'argument de celles que durant les troubles j'avois mises en lumiere'. This highly entertaining *Epistre au lecteur, par laquelle succintement l'autheur respond à ses calomniateurs,* is a denunciation of what appears to be a composite character, who incorporates all the vices of those who had attacked the poet during the civil war. This person, Ronsard argues, is an atheist — and a chameleon, who affects to support whichever party suits his advantage. And, Ronsard adds, he does actually know someone of that ilk, who had learned Calvinism in Lausanne and Geneva, had then derided Calvin and his doctrine — and then attacked him, Ronsard. Last sum-

mer, Ronsard adds, this individual showed him sonnets he had
written against Bèze (whom he now worships as a god), and
Ronsard has the original manuscript — from which he publishes
the following:

> S'armer du nom de Dieu et aucun n'en avoir,
> Prescher un Jesus Christ et nyer son essence,
> Gourmander tout un jour et prescher abstinence,
> Prescher d'amour divin et haine concevoir;
>   Prescher les cinq Canons sans faire leur vouloir,
> Paillarder librement et prescher continence,
> Prescher frugalité et faire grand despence,
> Prescher la charité et chascun decevoir;
>   Compter dessus les doigtz, faire bonne grimace,
> Amuser de babil toute une populace,
> Mignarder d'un clin d'œil le plus profond des Cieux;
>   Cacher souz le manteau d'une façon mauvaise
> Un vouloir obstiné, un cœur ambitieux,
> C'est la perfection de Theodore de Beze.

It is conceivable that Ronsard is the author of this sonnet, since
he omitted the text of the *Epistre* in which it is found from the
1578 edition of his *Œuvres,* while leaving the sonnet, thereby
implying that it was by him; and it was attributed to him when it
was reproduced, in 1582, in a collection of edifying poems, the
Muse chrestienne, published in Paris in 1582 (188). However,
he suppressed the poem from his 1584 edition of his works, and
in the *Epistre* he attributes the sonnet to a 'chrestien reformé',
which suggests the author may be Florent Chrestien (189).

(vii) Postwar attacks on Ronsard

Attacks on Ronsard by Reformers reached a crescendo in the
first civil war, understandably so in view of his role as defender
of the Catholic faith. But they continued after the war.

One Reformer who attacked Ronsard's work in these years
was Lambert Daneau who, in a letter of 7 March 1565 to Pierre
Daniel, declared: 'Such are the pitiful times we live in that
useless poems by Ronsard, some complaints or other to the

Queen, the King or goodness knows who, are no sooner written than they are put into print. But the most useful and excellent debates of the ancient theologians, and writings on morality, are despised' (190). Daneau probably had in mind poems such as Ronsard's *Compleinte à la Royne mere du Roy, La promesse* (also dedicated to the Queen Mother), and *Le procès,* addressed to the Cardinal of Lorraine: in all of these, he complains of lack of patronage (191).

Another Reformer, Albert Babinot, in a poem titled *Aux Muses sur les sainctes œuvres d'André de Rivaudeau,* published in 1568 in the edition of Rivaudeau's works, argued that Greek, Roman and French poets had defiled the Muses with salacious poetry, but that in recent times, several poets had been more enlightened — an implicit jibe at those who were not so 'enlightened' (and Ronsard was notorious among them, at least in huguenot mythology) (192).

Also in 1568, there appeared an appeal to Ronsard (and implicitly a reproach to him) by another Reformer, Charles Utenhove:

> Si tu me crois, Ronsard, des poetes la gloire,
> Des plus sçavans, Ronsard, le plus noble du sang,
> Des plus nobles du sang, justement mis au rang
> Des plus sçavans aussi par ta vertu notoire.
>
> Si tu me crois, Ronsard, tu changeras la Muse
> De ton divin esprit à chanter desormais
> Les louanges de Dieu plus que ne fis jamais,
> A chanter ce grand Roy personne ne s'abuse.
>
> L'ung chantera la paix, l'ung les champs et les bois,
> L'ung sonnera le loz du grand roy des François,
> Ou quelque demi-Dieu de ceste terre basse.
>
> Mais toy favorisé sur tous aultres des cieulx,
> Chanteras desormais le plus grand Dieu des Dieux,
> Qui tous dieux et tous rois, seul Dieu, seul roy surpasse.

The conciliatory tone of this poem reflects Utenhove's closeness to the Pléiade (193).

Ronsard is also the subject of an interesting attack on flattery by Innocent Gentillet, in his famous *Discours contre Machiavel,* of 1576:

> Au rang de ces Jangleurs [flatterers] peuvent bien estre mis à bon droit ces Poetes de nostre temps, qui par leurs poesies plaines de flatteries et de menteries, cerchent le moyen de crocheter quelque Abbaye ou quelque Prioré, ou bien d'avoir quelque don en recompense de leurs adulations. Je confesse bien que les Poëtes doyvent avoir plus de licence à escrire les louanges de quelqu'un, qu'un orateur ou historien: mais quand elles sont si hyperboliques, qu'elles reviennent plustost au deshonneur qu'à l'honneur de celuy de qui elles sont escrites, alors elles ne sont aucunement tolerables. Je prendray pour exemple les Epitaphes qui furent imprimez à Paris du feu Roy Charles IX peu après sa mort. Là où ces beaux Poetes disent, que le Roy devant que mourir avoit desfait plus de monstres, que jamais ne fit Hercules, ayant respandu tant de sang de ses sujets rebelles. Qu'il mourut comme Sanson, qui abbatit les colonnes qu'il embrassoit quand et soy, et que la justice, pieté, et religion, moururent en France quant et luy. Que la France luy a esté marastre ou noverque. Qu'il y avoit en luy un magazin de tous arts, et qu'il estoit fort expert aux mestiers mechaniques. Que le Roy Henry son frere à present regnant luy a succedé, comme Castor à Pollux, comme un Dieu à un autre Dieu. Que le Roy Charles est mort martyr de Jesus Christ, et qu'il doit estre doresnavant invoqué comme Sainct. Je vous prie, y a-il homme de jugement rassis, qui ne voye à l'œil, que tels propos sont plustost de gens transportez d'entendement, par une extreme affection de flaterie, que non pas de quelques gaillars Poetes, poussez d'un gentil esprit poetique? (194)

Although Gentillet does not name Ronsard, his target is clear from the fact that virtually all the examples he gives of flattery of Charles IX are found in Ronsard's *Tombeau du feu roy Tres-Chrestien Charles Neufiesme* (195).

Henri Estienne attacked the 'pagan' language of the Pléiade in his *Deux dialogues du nouveau language françois italianizé* (1578):

> [...] on use du mot *Fortune* au lieu de nommer Dieu. [...] Et aucuns (je ne sçay si c'est pour opposer la philosophie stoique à la religion christianique) font sonner fort haut, et à tous propos, *fatal* et *fatalité*, et *fatalement*, et *une fatale destinée*. Et viennent jusques à faire un verbe *fatalizer*. Quelques-uns disent aussi *le Ciel*, au lieu de dire Dieu... (196)

This is an issue on which contemporary debate was very lively. Montaigne, whose use of the word 'Fortune' initially worried a censor in Rome, defended the use of these poetic periphrases for divine power in *Des prieres*(197).

In 1579, François de L'Isle attacked 'Ronsard, Jodelle, Baïf et autres vilains poëtes' for supplanting Marot's psalm translations with their 'vilaines chansons et lascive musique' (198). And Yves Rouspeau published in 1581 a compilation of *Quatrains spirituels de l'honneste amour*. It begins with a poem titled *Louanges de l'amour divin, aux poëtes de ce temps:*

> Vous qui vous repaissez de fables poëtiques,
> Propres à vos cerveaux creux et melancoliques,
> Vous qui avez esté dès la jeunesse appris
> Es arts voluptueux de la belle Cypris...
>
> Qui n'avez autre but en composant des vers
> Sinon de contenter l'oreille des pervers....

In the same work, Rouspeau attacked Ronsard and Desportes:

> Fuyez Ronsard, et Desportes mignars
> Flatteurs de court, et maquereaux infames,
> De chasteté, qui est l'honneur des femmes,
> Grands ennemis, et amis des paillards (199).

We have already encountered Rouspeau as the author of a denunciation of poetry which extols false gods.

Finallly, Ronsard is one probable target of the biting attacks by Théodore Agrippa d'Aubigné on flattering court poets.

Among various passages, the following seems significant (the word 'Si' at the beginning has the sense of 'however'):

> Si, depuis quelque temps, les plus subtils esprits
> A deguiser le mal ont finement apris
> A nos princes fardez la trompeuse maniere
> De revestir le diable en ange de lumiere.
> Encore qu'à leurs repas ils facent disputer
> De la vertu, que nul n'oseroit imiter,
> Qu'ils recerchent le los des affetez poëtes,
> Quelques Sedecias, agreables prophetes [. . .]
> Tout cela n'a caché nos rudes veritez.

As can be seen, the point about the angel and the devil reproduces an earlier attack on Ronsard by Bèze; and the reference to disputations at mealtimes is an allusion to Henry III's practice of getting poets and scholars to debate issues of moral philosophy at court (indeed, the allusion may be to Ronsard's *Des vertus intellectuelles et morales* (200).

The civil war of 1562 seems to have polarised attitudes towards Ronsard. Whereas, before the war, many Catholics criticised him as a pagan or licentious or flattering poet, he now appears only to find unalloyed admiration among Catholics. Paul de Foix, in a letter to Queen Elizabeth's secretary, presented Ronsard as an opponent of flattery (201). Montaigne endorsed Ronsard's attack on the Reformers for converting the sacred text into 'chansons' (in *Des prieres*) and defended love poetry of which the work of Ronsard was the prime example (in *De la vanité*).

(viii)   Ronsard's reaction to the new attacks

Ronsard's response to the renewed clamour for Christian verse and to the attacks on his 'ecrits à la mode payenne' took two forms. One was to write further explicitly Christian poetry. Guy Lefèvre de La Boderie declared that some of the French bishops wanted to encourage Christian verse, and that they put the suggestion that it be written to some of the 'meilleurs de nos poetes, qui s'en seroient beaucoup mieux acquittez que moy' (202). Ronsard may well be among the poets who were approached in this way (especially after his services to the Church in 1562 and 1563). He translated the *Te Deum* into French verse, and dedicated all editions after the first to the Bishop of Valence, Jean de Monluc, 'pour chanter en son eglise' (203).

It is worth digressing momentarily to observe that Le Fèvre de La Boderie's *Encyclie des secrets de l'eternité*, published in Antwerp in 1570, reads as a comprehensive attempt to persuade the surviving poets of the Pléiade to turn their hand to Christian verse, and it contains denunciations of the three types of verse which, we have seen, most antagonised Reformers: writings about the pagan gods, erotic verse and flattering poetry. For example, a sonnet to Jean Vauquelin de La Fresnaye begins:

> Laisson, mon Vauquelin, ces vaines poësies
> Qui en noz jeunes ans nous ont tant delecté:
> Laisson ce fard grégeois, ce parler affecté,
> Et du viel Ascræan les fables ja moisies.
> Quiton du fol Amour les feintes courtoisies,
> Et ne vantons des grans qui ne l'ont merité:
> Mais celebrons de Dieu la pure verité,
> Ensuyvant des neuf cieus les neuf Muses choisies.

The volume contains many other poems on the same theme, but the tone is not hostile to Ronsard and the Pléiade. On the contrary, there are poems dedicated to Baïf, Tyard, Dorat, as well as a long *Hymne à Jesus-Christ nostre seigneur, de ses victoires et trionfes,* dedicated to Ronsard himself (204).

Ronsard's other way of responding to the clamour for Christian verse was to elaborate in much greater detail than hitherto the theory that pagan mythology can convey, allegorically, moral and religious truths. In 1561, he had expounded the theory in an *Elegie à Jacques Grevin* (205). After the war, he gave further explanations. In the *Hymne de l'Automne,* published in *Les trois livres du recueil des nouvelles poesies* of 1564, Ronsard tells how he was instructed in the art of poetry by Euterpe, and then by the scholar Jean Dorat who showed him how to 'feindre et cacher les fables', how to envelop the truth in a cloak of fables, a 'fabuleux manteau' (206). In the *Hymne de l'Hyver,* published in the same collection, he developed this idea, telling how 'philosophie' places a veil over the face of truth so that people will hold truth in awe, and feel the desire to get to know it better (207).

In the *Abbregé de l'Art poetique,* published in 1565, he wrote that the Muses are the daughters of Jupiter, and added, 'c'est à dire de Dieu, qui de sa saincte grace a premierement par elles faict cognoistre aux peuples ignorans les excellences de sa majesté'. Poets, in other words, were the earliest theologians, and theology was the earliest poetry: 'Car la poësie n'estoit au premier aage qu'une Theologie allegoricque, pour faire entrer au cerveau des hommes grossiers par fables plaisantes et colorées les secretz qu'ils ne pouvoient comprendre, quand trop ouvertement on leur descouvroit la verité' (208).

It is significant that all these explanations of the theory of the underlying sense of 'pagan' fables come after a decade in which Ronsard had been under sustained attack for 'paganism'; and most of them come after the sharp exchange of polemic in 1562–63. Ronsard had made many concessions to the demand for edifying verse, but he was not willing to sacrifice to the Reformers his attachment to the heritage of antiquity.

Ronsard did not simply outline the theory of the veiled meaning: he gave examples of fables of his that convey underlying messages. We have already seen him give hints, in the *Hymnes,* about the presence of an edifying dimension in the fables he tells: the labours of Hercules are prefigurations of events in the life of Christ; the torments of the underworld are representations of the pangs of ambtion. Now, after the controversies of 1563, he gives further and more explicit guidance to his readers. Paradoxically, of course: to spell out meanings which are intended to be veiled could be seen as undermining the essence of this means of communication. But Ronsard does so partly to vindicate his practice of veiling (and to refute the charge of paganism), and partly in the hope of developing some sensitivity in his more literally-minded readers, so that they will approach his other poems with a more open and receptive mind and a more imaginative disposition. It seems certain that there are veiled meanings in many poems in which Ronsard does not refer to veiling at all (209).

Thus, in the *Hymne de l'hyver,* after showing how philosophy encourages a love of truth by veiling her utterances, he adds that this poem itself is an example of the technique of veiling:

> Tel j'ay tracé cet hymne, imitant l'exemplaire
> Des fables d'Hesiode et de celles d'Homere.

The veiled content of the poem is a very clever reiteration of the attacks on Reformers he had published in 1562, as I have shown elsewhere: it was designed to circumvent a prohibition on the publication of polemical tracts (210).

In *Le Pin,* a poem published in 1569, Ronsard declares that the story of Atys, who castrated himself to join the devotees of Cybele, teaches that a philosopher must cut himself off from worldly pleasures to cultivate philosophy (211). A little later, in 1572, he published the first (and only) four books of his epic, the *Franciade,* and the reader is advised that there are allegorical dimensions to the work: he notes in a letter *Au lecteur* that in this epic, 'comme presque en tous autres poëtes', Juno represents 'une maligne necessité qui contredit souvent aux vertueux' (212).

And in a *Discours à Monsieur de Cheverny,* first published in 1584, he explains the fable of Jupiter's two privy councillors, Tantalus (who rashly revealed divine secrets to men and was thrust into the underworld) and Minos (who was discreet and reliable): it is a commentary on the relationship between a monarch and his servants (213). It seems distinctly possible that alongside this avowed meaning, there is another: for the poem echoes, in mythological language, a fundamental theme of the poems written overtly against the Reformers, that God's secrets must not be rashly revealed to the uncomprehending masses. Thus, Tantalus could well be a cypher for the Reformers.

To rely on one's readers to see an allusive message is to take a risk. In his famous prologue to *Gargantua,* Rabelais had first pointed out that his book had hidden meanings, and then warned that not every hidden meaning which had been discerned in books had been intended by their authors. Ronsard, for his part, had the (probably slightly unnerving) experience of seeing parts of his *Franciade* interpreted, ingeniously, as allusive attacks on the Court: the author of the famous *Reveille-matin des François* presented Ronsard's depiction of the corrupt Merovingian monarchs as a clever allusion to Catherine de Médicis and Charles IX and their responsibility for the St. Bartholomew's Day massacres (214). That Ronsard was prepared to take the risk of seeing his work traduced, and of being depicted as subversive, and at a time when he had many enemies, says much for his commitment to this type of writing. This type of discourse differs greatly from that of the Reformers, who saw theology as too important a matter to subject to risk of misinterpretation by their readers, and who wrote literally.

Thus, there are abundant statements in Ronsard both about the theory of veiling and about his practice of veiling. In fact, allusive discourse was so much a part of the cultural fabric that Ronsard may well have felt, especially in the early years of his career, that there was no need for him to say very much about this. The fact that his expositions of the theory of the hidden meaning are found predominantly in the years following his main controversy with the Reformers suggests that he wanted to show that apparent 'paganism' could carry an edifying *altior sensus*. Indeed, it could carry it in a specifically Christian way, for Christian teaching was originally conveyed in parables...

CHAPTER VI

Bèze's continuing salvoes

(i) Bèze defends his poetry

Bèze's *Poemata* of 1548 had been roundly castigated by Catholic polemicists. Some of his Catholic foes, such as Joachim Du Bellay, made deductions about his personal life from the content of these poems. And in 1562, when Bèze's standing as a Reformer was at its height in France, Ronsard had disobligingly recalled Bèze's role as a love poet. Bèze was stung. This is clear from his rejoinder to a Catholic polemicist, Claude de Sainctes (215).

It is also clear from a letter of 1 September 1568 to a Hungarian bishop recently converted to the Reformation, Andrea Dudithius (or Dudycz). There, Bèze states that he is going to republish his youthful poems, which his detractors have used as the basis for slanders against him; some of these poems, he admits, are hardly Christian works, but they are fictional and cannot be used as a basis for conclusions about his way of life; and his enemies reproach him for things which, in others, they regard as virtues (almost certainly an allusion to the writing of love poetry) (216). Bèze was to republish this letter in 1573, in his *Epistolæ theologicæ*. It is probably no accident that it was to Dudithius that Bèze chose to address these thoughts: for Dudithius had been a pupil of Dorat in Paris, and (it is thought) had almost certainly been an acquaintance of Ronsard (217).

The letter to Dudithius gives a foretaste of a more important document, the preface (also dedicated to Dudithius) to the second edition of the *Poemata,* which was published in Geneva by Henri Estienne in 1569. It is clear that the dispute with the Pléiade poets was as important to Bèze as it had ever been:

> Et ut ad poetas descendam, quos ipsi poetas his viginti annis excuderunt? quos in deliciis habent? quos in cælum efferunt? Quum cuiusdam Oliva, quum eiusdem epigrammata Latina, quibus inter cætera sacræ virginis raptum describit (cuius alioqui doctrinæ et ingenio nihil detractum velim) quum alterius, melioris sane poetæ quam viri, amores, præfixa etiam Cassandræ seu fictitiæ (sic enim potius arbitrari malo) seu veræ scortatricis, seu adulteræ, imagine, quum alia eiusdem innumerabilia pene carmina ederentur (edi autem etiamnum quotidie, nec quicquam per compita vulgarius illic circumferri, ne ipsi quidem inficiabuntur) — quando tamen istorum quispiam intercessit? quum vel senatus, vel regium quoque privilegium illis scriptis præfigitur, quis istorum hoc reprehendit? quosnam libellos, et iuvenes et senes, pueri, virgines, viri, mulieres illic manibus terunt? Quid? quosnam alios conduxerunt qui Calvino et Bezæ gratis maledicerent? et iidem illi ad maledicendum conducti, annon hodie pinguissimas quasque Abbatias et Episcopatus iis ipsis venantur et consequuntur, quæ vere et re ipsa patrata, tam patienter in illis ferunt, tam severe in nobis vel ficta reprehendunt? (218)

> ['And to come to poets, which poets have these people printed these last twenty years? Whom do they find delightful? Whom do they praise to the skies? When the Olive of one of them, when the same person's Latin epigrams, in which among other things he describes the rape of a vestal virgin (I do not wish in other respects to detract from his learning and intellect); when the love poems of another, who is certainly more of a good poet than a good man, which are prefaced by the picture of a Cassandra who is either ficititious (as I prefer to believe) or a real whore, or adulteress, when other almost innumerable poems by the same man are published (and they

are published even now every day, nor is there anything
which is more commonly circulated on street corners, nor
are they themselves more commonly corrupted) — when
did any of them protest? When, moreover, these writings
are prefaced by a permission to print from the *Parlement*
or from kings, which of them criticised that? What kind
of books are young and old, boys, girls, men and women
wearing away by use? What? Did they not put together
other books which gratuitously insult Calvin and Bèze?
And those same people, having been drawn into slander, do they not today hunt after and track down the
best-endowed abbeys and bishoprics? And when these
people have really and truly perpetrated such deeds, are
not their fellow-countrymen as ready to tolerate them as
they are to reproach us severely for similar deeds, even
imaginary ones?']

The reference to poetry published twenty years ago is to the
earliest publications of Ronsard and Du Bellay and their followers. Interestingly (and, surely, disingenuously), Bèze again
condemns Du Bellay's implicitly evangelical *Olive*. He then
turns to Ronsard, deploring the *Amours* of 1552; and when he
censures both Du Bellay and Ronsard for their 'other books
which slander Calvin and Bèze gratuitously' he was probably
thinking of Du Bellay's 1552 attack on him and of Ronsard's
poems of 1562 – 63.

In the same preface, Bèze goes on to deride Du Bellay's
defence of the *Amadis* novels (which had appeared, as we saw,
in Du Bellay's sharp rejoinder to the preface to *Abraham*):

> Extant Gallicæ quædam nugæ ex Hispano sermone con-
> versæ, et crassis aliquot voluminibus vix comrehensæ,
> quas Amadin Gallicum appellant: iis nihil præcipue
> præter turpissimos et fœdissimos amores narratur, et ita
> quidem ut res ipsæ oculis pene subiiciantur. Quænam
> vero tandem familiæ libris illis carent? Immo non ali-
> unde iidem illi qui sic in Bezam plenis buccis declami-
> tant, linguæ Gallicæ puritatem discere se gloriantur. Uti
> superioribus annis alius non minus impurus scriptor,
> quem Peregrinum vocabant, in cœnobiis proponi tan-
> quam eloquentiæ exemplar solebat.

['There exist certain frivolities in French, translated from the Spanish, and so extensive that thick tomes scarcely contain them, which they call "Amadis de Gaule". The content of these volumes is almost exclusively the foulest and filthiest love stories, and so much so that these things can scarcely be set before your eyes. But which household does not have its own copies of those books? Moreover, those people who keep on shouting invective at Bèze, claim that they have learned the pure French language from no other source than these books. Just as, in years gone by, a no less filthy writer called Peregrinus was set forth in monasteries as an example of eloquence']

The scathing allusion to those who attack Bèze and present the *Amadis* translations as a model of French expression echoes the content, cited above, of Du Bellay's *Ode au Seigneur Des Essars, sur le discours de son Amadis,* of 1552. Clearly, Bèze was as badly stung by Du Bellay as Du Bellay had been by him. I do not know who the Peregrinus is who is alluded to in the last sentence of this quotation.

Bèze continues:

Delias scilicet, Neæras, Olivas, Cassandras, Sideridas boni Cacolyci ferre possunt, et assiduos illorum decantatores, Abbates et Episcopos salutare: Bezam vero, qui nonnulla iuvenis luserit, quæ a suis accusatoribus prius collaudata ipsemet primus palam et scriptis et reipsa ultro damnarit, ut omnium hominum impurissimum, egregii pudicitiæ vindices ferre non possunt. At patimini saltem castissimi homines, aliquem resipiscentibus peccatoribus et meretricibus locum in regno cælorum tribui.

['The good Catholics are plainly able to tolerate the Délies, and Neæras, and Olives, and Cassandras, and Sideridas, and to pay their respects to those abbots and bishops who are the assiduous poets who extol them. But Bèze, who amused himself by writing some things when he was a young man, which were originally praised by his accusers, and who is himself the first to condemn them openly, in writing and in fact, and without anyone asking him to — these defenders of the highest morality cannot tolerate him, as though he were the most impure of all men. But, oh most chaste of men! At least allow some place in the kingdom of heaven for repentant sinners and whores']

As Bèze's editors have pointed out, the allusions are to the heroines of verse by (successively) Scève, Marullus, Du Bellay, Ronsard and Baïf (219). This preface was also to appear in the third edition of Bèze's poems, probably published by Estienne in Geneva in 1576 (220).

(ii)   The 'Histoire ecclesiastique' of 1580

It is uncertain whether and to what extent Bèze can be credited with the Reformers' *Histoire ecclesiastique* of 1580. It seems that he assembled some of the material which went into it, and supervised its production (221). The book attacks Ronsard, resurrecting various charges levelled at him by Reformers in 1563, and underlining an allegation that he had engaged in armed confrontation with Reformers:

> Pierre Ronsard, gentilhomme doué de grandes graces en la poësie françoise entre tous ceux de nostre temps, mais au reste ayant loué sa langue pour non seulement souiller sa veine de toutes ordures, mais aussi mesdire de la Religion et de tous ceux qui en font profession, s'estant fait prestre, se voulut mesler en ces combats avec ses compagnons. Et pour cest effect, ayant assemblé quelques soldats en un village nommé d'Evaillé, dont il estoit curé, fit plusieurs courses avec pilleries et meurtres. Cela contraignit ceux du pays [i.e. the local Reformers] de rappeler leurs soldats qui estoient au Mans, lesquels à leur retour se jetterent dans l'abbaye de S. Calais, tenans ceux qui y estoient en telle sujetion, que cependant les moines n'estoient empeschés en leur service, ni d'aller et venir. Mais abusans de ceste liberté, quelques uns d'iceux, [...] le vingt-huictiesme jour de May (1562), estans allés à Conflans, marchanderent avec certain nombre de seditieux de venir massacrer leurs hostes, le jour qu'ils appellent leur Sacre ou Feste Dieu, leur assignans

> l'heure du premier coup de vespres; ce qu'ils executerent
> à la façon des vespres Siciliennes [. . .] (222).

This is an elaboration of a charge first made in one of the 1563
pamphlets against Ronsard, the anonymous *Remonstrance à la
Royne*. Neither this pamphlet, nor the *Histoire ecclesiastique*
(which is probably the source of later historians' accounts of
Ronsard's supposed armed skirmishes with the Reformers) car-
ries conviction on this point (223). It is probable that this
presentation of Ronsard as a warrior priest is a rejoinder to the
poet's deprecation of Bèze's 'Evangile armée'.

(iii)   Bèze renews the attack

A poem in a later edition of Bèze's *Poemata* seems to be directed pre-eminently at Ronsard. It bears the title *In quosdam
poetas* ['Against certain poets'] and reads:

> Ipse mihi doctum si dictet carmen Apollo,
> Sic tamen abstrusis obscurum sensibus illud,
> Ut vario abductum lectorem errore fatiget,
> Hunc tandem fructu non exæquante laborem,
> Excipiam invitus Phœbi dictata magistri.
>   At cui vel suavi conditum nectare carmen
> Pangere posse datum, puro castoque lepore
> Demulcens pariter mentem lectoris et aures,
> Argutum aut cuius lector miretur acumen,
> Vel quod grande sonans secum super astra legentem
> Attollat, cælique beet velut arce receptum,
> Vel quod non fatuo teretes sale defricet aures,
> Et cieat torpens moderato ardore palatum,
> Illimis semper, puraque argenteus unda,
> Nec scopulis horrens ullis, ceu volvitur amnis,
> Invitans, satiansque sitim potantis abunde:
> Hic mihi sit verus tum re, tum nomine, vates.
>   Vos autem Aonidum sanctum temerare pudorem
> Et puros ausi latices turbare petulci,
> Ingrati procul ite, procul: vel crimina fassi,
> Discite vos castis et vestra dicare Camœnis.
>   At vos, ô rauca stridentes voce cicadæ,

Vana coaxantes tumido vos gutture ranæ,
Vos fatuo elumbes vomitantes pectore versus,
Sensa quibus nec mens, nec voces suggerit œstrum,
Quis sacro vatum dignetur nomine sanus?

['If Apollo himself dictates a learned poem to me, but
in such a way that it is obscure and has an abstruse
meaning, so that it wearies the reader who has been hin-
dered by its meandering deceptions, and at the end of
the day the labour of reading it is not equalled by any
benefit, I should be reluctant to accept what the master
Phœbus had dictated to me. But anyone who has the
gift of composing a song seasoned with sweet nectar,
and which allures the mind and the ears of the reader
with its pure and chaste graciousness, or one which the
reader admires for its sharp subtlety, or which with its
strong sound bears the reader with it beyond the stars,
and which rewards the reader, conveying him as it were
into the citadel of heaven, or which caresses elegant ears
with a wit which is not devoid of purpose, and which
rouses a jaded palate with a well-tuned ardour, always
lucid, and which rolls along like a clear, silvery stream
with no rocks in it, and which feasts the reader, gen-
crously slaking his thirst — let this be the true poet for
me, in name and in reality. But you wantons who have
the effrontery to despise the holy modesty of the Muses
and to disturb the pure waters, be off, be off, for you
are ungrateful; or, confess to your crimes, and learn to
dedicate yourselves and your talents to the Muses. But
you, cicadas, hissing with a raucous voice, you frogs
who croak inanities from your swollen throats, you who
vomit lifeless verses from your insipid minds, in whom
intellect prompts no ideas and inspiration prompts no ut-
terance — who in his right mind would dignify you with
the sacred title of "poet"?']

The attack on obscurity and obscenity suggests Ronsard is his
target, and the allusion in the concluding lines to the croaking
of frogs echoes, perhaps deliberately, the confrontation of 1563
between Ronsard and Reformers (224).

(iv)   The death of Ronsard, and after

The denunciations of Ronsard's alleged paganism, licentiousness and flattery continued throughout his lifetime. And in
1584, a complete edition of his early collection of erotic verses,
the *Folastries,* appeared — doubtless produced by Reformers to
compromise their great foe (similarly, a 1600 edition of Bèze's
Poemata juvenilia seems to have been published to discredit
the Reformer).

At the time of his death, his panegyrists hailed him as a
hero of the Catholic Reformation; and his reputation as a con-
troversialist was to persist long after his death (225). But his
admirers were on the defensive where his love poetry was concerned (226). One of his panegyrists, George Crichton, wrote
as follows in a funerary oration on the poet:

> The one thing about his work which is condemned is
> that he wrote some poems dealing with love. as though
> those were the vices of the man and not of the age we
> live in, and as though it were not the case that all poets
> let themselves go a bit in their youth, and consequently
> some of their work has to be cut out. But anyway, what
> do those books of love poems of Ronsard have which
> could not be recited among a troop of maidens? Are
> there any lascivious or immodest lines? Certainly not.
> And would that those who say these things had deserved
> as well of the Catholic Church as he who is tainted with
> this stain of insult without any blame of his own (227).

The famous Jesuit scholar, Antonio Possevino, declared in
1593: 'Among the French, Peter Ronsard stood out, especially
in those French poems which he directed at the Calvinists; for
his writings about love are most unworthy of the eyes and ears
of Christians' (228).

Another interesting commentator on this issue is Montaigne,
who probably had in mind the various attacks on Ronsard in
the following passage (from *Sur des vers de Virgile*):

> Qui ostera aux Muses les imaginations amoureuses,
> leur desrobera le plus bel entretien qu'elles ayent et

> la plus noble matiere de leur ouvrage; et qui fera
> perdre à l'amour la communication et service de la
> poësie, l'affoiblira de ses meilleures armes; par ainsin
> on charge le dieu d'accointance et de bien vueillance et
> les deesses protectrices de l'humanité et de justice, du
> vice d'ingratitude et de mesconnoissance.

Elsewhere (in *De la vanité*), Montaigne castigated Bèze:

> J'ay veu en ma jeunesse un galant homme presenter
> d'une main au peuple des vers excellens en beauté et
> en desbordement, et de l'autre main la plus quereleuse
> reformation theologienne de quoy le monde se soit
> desjeuné il y a long temps.

Like so many other commentators, Montaigne refrains from naming his target, but contemporaries would have had little difficulty identifying the Reformer, given the notoriety of his early poems.

There is further criticism of Ronsard on another topic in the preface to a work titled *La Christiade*, by Jean d'Escorbiac, a nephew of Guillaume du Bartas. Escorbiac's work was apparently written around 1590, although it was not published until 1612. Addressing his readers, Escorbiac writes of his poem: 'il n'est point paré de ces belles et riches fleurs de bien-dire, vous n'y orrez point ces oracles, ces aenigmes, ces pointes relevées, ces paronamases recherchées par ces rares et divins esprits qui decorent la France en ce siecle. Nostre Sauveur (l'humilité mesme) ne demande qu'une simplicité' (229).

(v) Conclusion

We have seen that in the course of his career, Ronsard made many concessions to his critics: he wrote explicitly Christian and edifying verse, made wide use of biblical passages in his political work, and guided the reader towards the veiled and edifying sense commonly to be found beneath the veil of allegory. He may have been asked to compose liturgical works, and he translated the *Te Deum*. The first posthumous edition contains, among the *Hymnes*, two new ones dedicated to saints (230).

These facts lend weight to the assertion by Claude Binet, in his *Vie de Ronsard,* that the poet would have written several more Christian works had he survived longer (231). It is clear that Ronsard had no qualms about meeting demand for Christian verse.

We noted a *rapprochement* between Ronsard and his friends on the other side of the religious divide shortly before the outbreak of the first civil war. While the succession of wars did nothing to improve the climate between Ronsard and Reformers, and while Bèze seems never to have lost the cutting edge of his resentment of the poet, the two sides converged, interestingly, in collections of edifying verse published in the 1580s. While one can attribute given anthologies unambiguously to Reformers or to Catholics, there are several such anthologies which, as has been shown, contain poems by people of the 'other' persuasion. Thus, a collection of *Cantiques* published by the Reformer, Estienne L'Huillier, *sieur* de Maisonfleur, contains in its 1586 edition (amidst an assortment of poems by Reformers), Ronsard's translation of the *Te Deum* — which Ronsard had included in editions of his work among the *Discours,* his anti-Reformation poems (232)! A few years later, this compilation evolved into *Les Cantiques du sieur de Valagre, et les Cantiques du sieur de Maizonfleur*: the 1592 edition of this work brought in three further poems by Ronsard — the *Hymne triomphal de Marguerite de Valois,* the *Hercule chrestien,* and *Sur le trespas du roi Charles neufiesme* ('Si le grain de forment ne se pourrist en terre'). As has been pointed out, the inclusion of these poems, and notably the *Hercule chrestien* which had been so vigorously attacked by some Reformers, seems to indicate that old feuds were waning (233).

We have seen, too, that before the civil war sharpened the divisions and gave Ronsard a high profile as a Catholic poet, calls for Christian verse and deprecations of his 'paganism' emanated from Catholics and Reformers alike. Such differences between Catholics and Reformers as we have seen are of a cultural kind (Catholics, and certainly Ronsard, seem more ready to embrace the classical heritage in a syncretist manner), or a 'political', opportunist kind (the barrage of opposition to Ronsard's 'paganism' from Reformers became much more intense after 1562, when he became involved in polemic with them, and Catholics' criticisms of him much more muted). There is no doctrinal difference between Reformers and Catholics on the question of the desirability of Christian verse; and this would explain why Ronsard had no difficulty in making the concessions he did.

There is no better illustration of the convergence of Catholics and Reformers on this point than in an attack on paganism published by a leading Jesuit in 1600:

> Certes, pour dire cecy en passant, c'est une misere autant digne de compassion que de honte, que plusieurs poëtes et orateurs parmy les Chrestiens, et nommément en nostre France, employent la bonté et fertilité de leurs esprits, à escrire des comptes, des fables, des amours et autres choses ou inutiles, ou pernicieuses, et s'esvantrent comme araignés à tistre des filets aux mouches et œuvres de vanité, quittant mille beaux subjects sur lesquels ils pourroient avec loüange eternelle faire courir la poincte de leur style. C'est une grande honte au nom Chrestien de voir un Pindare payen, un Euripide, un Virgile, un Appelles, un Philostrate et sembables aucteurs prophanes, travailler si soigneusement à descrire, chanter, peindre et representer leurs capitaines, leurs gestes, leurs dieux, leurs vices et leurs vanitez, pour la gloire de leur superstition, et plusieurs Chrestiens ne sçavoir choisir ny une matiere ny une façon propre du nom Chrestien, pour escrire chrestiennement à la louange du vray Dieu, à l'honneur et lustre de leur religion.

In reading these lines by Louis Richeome (234), one is reminded of Bèze's denunciation of Ronsard, Du Bellay and Peletier, with which our story began.

The sharpness of the exchanges we have been examining did not prevent a high degree of mutual respect between the protagonists. While the content of poetry by Ronsard and Du Bellay met with disapproval from Reformers, its excellence met with approval and emulation. Thus, work by both of them was redeployed (without their permission, needless to say, and without their approval) to serve the cause of the Reformation. A case in point is Du Bellay's collection of poems on ancient Rome, the *Antiquitez* (and its companion-collection, the *Songe*), which was reissued in English, French, Flemish and German versions in a strongly anti-papal work titled *A Theatre for Worldlings*; the English translation, by Edmund Spenser, adroitly alters those passages in which Du Bellay endorses papal supremacy (235). In a similar way, Agrippa d'Aubigné was an admirer of Ronsard and, although no-one seems to have examined the extent of his indebtedness, apparently owes much to Ronsard (236). Du Bellay's religious poems, and Ronsard's, were exploited by Odet de la Noue in *L'Uranie, ou nouveau recueil de chansons spirituelles et chrestiennes,* published in Geneva in 1591 (237). And Ronsard was to maintain repeatedly in his 1562–63 pamphlets, and with justification, that the Reformers, in writing against him, had plagiarised him (238).

Confrontation did not exclude a courteous and indeed cordial relationship between poets on opposing sides of the religious divide. Unfortunately, it is impossible to say precisely what views Ronsard and Bèze held of each other as persons. But we have seen the excellent relations that Ronsard and Des Masures enjoyed, and this was not unique. Florent Chrestien appears to have become reconciled with Ronsard after the sharp exchange of 1563, and Ronsard praises him in the posthumously-published preface to the *Franciade* (the reconciliation may owe something to Chrestien's return to the Catholic faith) (239). Paul Melissus, the committed Reformer and admirer of Ronsard, remained faithful to Ronsard to the end (240). Melissus had lived in Geneva for three years, and in Italy from 1577–80, especially in Rome, where his relationships with Catholic authorities were excellent. Melissus's excellent biographer has described this as surprising, but it is not: it seems that individuals who refrained from proselytising zeal could quite happily exist in areas controlled by religious foes (think of Montaigne in Germany) (241).

Notes

Note: In the case of some frequently-cited works, abbreviated bibliographical information only is given here: for full details, please see the Bibliography.

(1) See P. Laumonier, *Ronsard poète lyrique*, 2*e* éd., Paris, 1923, p. 23.

(2) The passage reads:

> Ce nom d'Ode a etè introduit de notre tans, par Pierre de Ronsard: auquel ne falhirè de temoignage, que lui etant ancor an grand'jeunece, m'an montra quelques unes de sa façon, an notre vile du Mans: e me dit delors, qu'il se proposoèt ce g'anre d'ecrire à l'imitacion d'Horace, comme depuis il a montrè à tous les Françoes, e ancor plus par sus sa premiere intancion, à l'imitacion du premier des Liriques, Pindare.

(Ed. A. Boulanger, Paris, 1930, p. 172 – 174).

(3) See *In Euclidis elementa geometrica demonstrationum libri sex,* Lugduni, 1557, B.L. 8548 f 20, 2ro-3ro:

> Scis quanti te semper fecerim, mi Ronsarde. Me vero abs te non parvi fieri exploratum habeo. Nam et amicitiæ nostræ memoriam mutuo testimonio posteritati prodidimus, quod certe ad vitam ipsam non parum affert

momenti: habet enim ea publica confirmatio singularem quandam delectationem. Sed et ad me valde pertinere arbitror (neque te aliter esse affectum existimo) ut omnis ætas intelligat, nos non modo temporum, sed etiam animorum coniunctione copulatos fuisse. [. . .] Scis enim quanta fuerit dudum inter nos studiorum consensio et conciliatio, ex quo tempore etiam nobis tertius adscriptus est Joachimus Bellaius [. . .] Memini, quum esses etiamnum adolescens, me aliquot annis superiorem quanta benevolentia observares, Musarum nomine [. . .]

(4) On Peletier's links with the young Ronsard and Du Bellay, see C. Jugé, *Jacques Peletier Du Mans,* Paris, Le Mans, 1907, p. 22 – 34.

(5) See *L'Olive,* ed. E. Caldarini, Genève, 1974, p. 44.

(6) The poem, titled *A la ville du Mans,* was an epilogue to Peletier's book. For the text, see Du Bellay's *Œuvres poétiques,* ed. H. Chamard (v. 1 – 6) and Geneviève Demerson (v. 7, 8), Paris, S.T.F.M., 1908 – 1985, V, p. 235 – 236. This edition is referred to henceforth as 'Du Bellay, S.T.F.M.'

(7) See Jugé, p. 26 – 32.

(8) See Peletier's *Dialogue de l'Ortografe* of January 1550 (1551 n.s.) (the passage is cited in full by P.F. Geisendorf, *Théodore de Bèze,* Genève, 1949, p. 16 – 17). I am here drawing on Natalie Davis's 'Peletier and Beza part company', *Studies in the Renaissance,* XI, 1964, p. 188 – 222. She deals with the meetings in the Vascosan circle, where the other two regulars were Jean Martin and Denis Sauvage, on p. 188, 190 and 192 – 193.

(9) Vascosan published the *Epithalame d'Antoine de Bourbon et Janne de Navarre* and *L'Hymne de France,* both of 1549; he also printed (for Guillaume Cavellat, who published these works) Ronsard's *Quatre premiers livres des Odes* and *Ode de la paix,* both of 1550.

(10) Quoted from T. Thomson, 'The *Poemata* of Théodore de Bèze', in I.D. McFarlane, *ed., Acta Conventus neo-Latini Sanctandreani,* Binghamton, New York, 1986 (p. 409–415), p. 410.

(11) See Ronsard's *Œuvres complètes,* ed. P. Laumonier, I. Silver and R. Lebègue, 20 v., Paris, S.T.F.M., 1914–75, III, p. 183; IV, p. 33; V, p. 38; VII, p. 37, 56. Laumonier maintained (V, p. 41, n. 3) that the end of *Folastrie VI* is an imitation of Bèze's Elegy VII in the *Poemata* This edition is referred to henceforth as 'Ronsard, S.T.F.M.'.

(12) According to G.H. Tucker, *The Poet's Odyssey,* p. 10, Bèze's *Elegia* VI, l. 11–12 (*Poemata,* Paris, 1548, p. 27) was echoed in Du Bellay's *Olive,* s. 45; he also (p. 11) discerns possible echoes of Bèze in the *Antiquitez* and the *Songe.*

(13) See *Amores,* 24 (Du Bellay, S.T.F.M., VII, p. 156–159).

(14) 'Ce fut une belle guerre que l'on entreprit lors contre l'ignorance, dont j'attribue l'avantgarde à Seve, Beze et Pelletier, ou si le voulez autrement, ce furent les avantcoureurs des autres poëtes. Après, se meirent sur les rangs Pierre de Ronsard vendomois, et Joachim Du Bellay angevin [...]' (VI, vii; p 739 in the Paris, 1611 edition   B.L. 596 g 4).

(15) On Ronsard's denunciations of the 'vilain monstre Ignorance' and their meaning, see Laumonier's note in his *Ronsard poète lyrique,* 2e éd., Paris, 1923, p. 19, n. 6 and p. 64, n. 3.

(16) Du Bellay, S.T.F.M., IV, p. 9–10.

(17) Lutetiæ, B.L. 11403 aaa 35, p. 51. See my 'Théodore de Bèze and Philænus', *Bibliothèque d'Humanisme et Renaissance,* LII, 1990, p. 345–353.

(18) See the *Deffence et illustration,* ed. H. Chamard, Paris (S.T.F.M.), 1948, p. 86 and 67; and my 'Joachim Du Bellay défenseur d'Etienne Dolet', in K.A. Kuczynski, Z.J. Nowak and H. Tadeusiewicz, eds., *Munera philologica Georgio Starnawski ab amicis collegis discipulis oblata,* Lódz, 1992, p. 141–147.

(19) On this, see H. Meylan, 'La conversion de Bèze ou les longues hésitations d'un humaniste chrétien', in his *D'Erasme à Théodore de Bèze,* Genève, 1987, p. 145 – 167.

(20) See Ronsard, S.T.F.M., III, p. 95. In all editions after the first, the allusion to 'fraudes rommaines' is absent.

(21) See, for example, a poem *Sur le papat de Paule IIII* (endorsing that Pope's attempt to reform the Church), and his *Ecclesiæ querimonia* (in Du Bellay, S.T.F.M., V, p. 342 – 348 and VIII, p. 132 – 135 respectively).

(22) See his *Remonstrance au peuple de France,* l. 211 – 214 (p. 116 in my edition of his *Discours des miseres,* Genève, 1979). While Ronsard knew the Reformers' doctrines, there is no evidence he ever sympathised with them (see my note at this point in the edition).

(23) See Davis, 'Peletier and Beza part company', p. 194.

(24) Nicolaï's comment is in a letter of 18 December 1549: 'Audio hominem ex Galliis profugisse ad Helvetios, neque tamen caussam fugæ intellexi: suspicor autem invidiam sibi conflasse, eo epigrammate, quo Doletum celebrat, hominem atheum, Parisiis iudico publico concrematum. Quod epigramma utinam non edidisset' (cited by M. Magnien in his edition of G. Colletet's *Vie d'Etienne Dolet,* Genève, 1992, p. 55, n. 83).

(25) See A. Bernus, *Théodore de Bèze à Lausanne,* Lausanne, 1900, p. 19. The sentence was not carried out, and in 1564 Bèze was able to have it rescinded: see his *Correspondance,* V, p. 178 – 179.

(26) See Davis, 'Peletier and Beza part company', p. 201 – 202; she notes that a possible motive for his departure is disillusionment with Vascosan, whose typesetters had failed to use his orthography in printing his *Œuvres poetiques* in 1547 (he arranged for his next works to be published by the Marnef brothers in Poitiers). Davis discusses Peletier's religious position in p. 205 – 211, concluding (p. 208) that 'Peletier shows evidence of Protestant sentiments; but either he toned them down

out of prudence or they were not very strong to begin with'. Jugé argued that 'entouré d'amis protestants et de protecteurs qui inclinaient à la réforme, Peletier, sans devenir agressif ou ligueur, garde les croyances traditionnelles' — *Jacques Peletier du Mans (1517 – 1582), Paris, Le Mans, 1907, p. 6.* He noted (p. 61) that in 1580, Peletier was accused by one Mauricius Bressius in Paris of being a Reformer: this is known from Peletier's *In Mauricium Bressium Apologia,* Paris, 1580. He also observed (p. 61, n. 1) that in *Scaligerana* (Cologne, 1695), there is a reference to 'Pelettarius [. . .] varius et inconstans in religione'. Jugé noted that Peletier denied the charge, though the denial seems to me less than totally unequivocal. See also Jugé, p. 87 – 91.

(27) *Deffence et illustration,* ed. Chamard (S.T.F.M.), p. 180.

(28) See Ronsard, S.T.F.M., I, 44, 46 and 82 – 83 respectively.

(29) Marot's psalm translations can be read in the edition by S.J. Lenselink, *Les Psaumes de Clément Marot,* Assen, Kassel, 1969, or in Marot's *Œuvres complètes,* ed. C.A. Mayer, VI, Les traductions, Genève, 1980.

(30) Jacques Peletier, we have seen, tells us that Ronsard first used the term 'ode' in France. But, Peletier added, the genre had been invented by Clément Marot, whose psalm translations were true odes, except that they lacked the name (*Art poëtique,* ed. A. Boulanger, Paris, 1930, p. 176; although the work was not published until 1555, it is plausible that Ronsard was familiar with Peletier's view). According to Laumonier, 'Peletier a voulu donner là une leçon de modestie au chef de la Pléiade, car il insiste sur l'importance lyrique des Psaumes avec quelque dureté pour Ronsard, qui avait affecté d'en parler assez légèrement et pour ainsi dire par manière d'acquit' (*Ronsard poète lyrique,* 2e éd., Paris, 1923, p. xlviii, citing Marty-Laveaux's *Appendice de la Pléiade française,* I, p. 7 – 8).

(31) Ronsard, S.T.F.M., I, 43.

(32) See Ronsard, S.T.F.M., I, 44–45; I, 77; I, 110; I, 72 respectively.

(33) See Ronsard, S.T.F.M., I, p. 31, 43, 44, 130, 163, 176; II, p. 106; V, 260. He pointed out in the preface to the *Odes* of 1550 that he had written many of these poems a long time ago. The claim to have invented the ode was also made by Du Bellay, and the respective claims of the two of them, and of Marot, have been discussed by several scholars. H. Chamard upheld Ronsard's claim (see 'L'invention de l'ode et le différend de Ronsard et de Du Bellay', *Revue d'Histoire Littéraire de la France*, VI, 1899, p. 21–54). Laumonier favoured Marot's claim: see *Ronsard poète lyrique*, 2e éd., Paris, 1923, p. xiv. C. Maddison concluded (convincingly, in my view) that although the claim of Ronsard and Du Bellay to have invented the French ode is not literally true, they 'publicised a term and a brand of poetry little known in French before, and theirs has been the lasting contribution' (*Apollo and the Nine, a history of the ode*, London, 1960, p. 205). I think the celebrated 'quarrel' between Du Bellay and Ronsard over the invention of the ode was stage-managed to deflect attention from the claim of Marot.

(34) Much earlier, 'David était devenu le symbole d'une inspiration spirituelle hostile au style païen': the idea goes back to Jerome and Augustine. See Guy Demerson, *La Mythologie classique dans l'œuvre lyrique de la Pléiade*, Genève, 1972, p. 254.

(35) '[...] ne voiant en nos poëtes françois chose qui fust suffisante d'imiter, j'allai voir les étrangers, et me rendi familier d'Horace, contrefaisant sa naive douceur, dès le méme temps que Clement Marot (seulle lumiere en ses ans de la vulgaire poësie) se travailloit à la poursuite de son Psautier, et osai le premier des nostres, enrichir ma langue de ce nom Ode' (Ronsard, S.T.F.M., I, p. 44).

(36) Du Bellay, *Deffence*, ed. H. Chamard, 1948, p. 40 and n. 3.

(37) Bèze, *Correspondance,* I, p. 200 – 201.

(38) The first sonnet in *L'Olive* expresses the aim of making Olive the equal of the *laurier immortel* (that is, of Petrarch's Laura). In the 1549 preface, Du Bellay declared he had imitated Petrarch, and the point is underlined by eulogies of Du Bellay by Dorat and Macrin published in the collection. In his *Deffence et illustration de la langue françoyse* (II, iv), Du Bellay presented Petrarch as the model for writers of sonnets. Bèze had earlier expressed hostility to licentious love poetry in an epigram dedicated to his friend Maclou Popon: see F. Aubert, J. Boussard, H. Meylan, 'Un premier recueil de poésies latines de Théodore de Bèze', *Bibliothèque d'Humanisme et Renaissance,* XV, 1953, p. 170.

(39) The fool's cap, usually bedecked with bells, was worn by jesters. See E. Welsford, *The Fool: his social and literary history,* London, 1935, p. 121 – 124.

(40) On Ronsard conferring 'divine' status on French kings, see my 'Ronsard et ses critiques contemporains', in *Ronsard en son quatrième centenaire,* cd. Y. Bellenger *et al.,* Genève, 1988, p. 83 and notes 4 and 5. He seems to have anticipated criticisms of the kind levelled by Bèze, for he argued in the preface to the odes that 'c'est le vrai but d'un poëte Liriq de celebrer jusques à l'extremité celui qu'il entreprend de louer' (S.T.F.M., I, p. 48). For denunciations of flattery at the time, see R.J. Clements, *Critical Theory and Practice of the Pléiade,* New York, 1970, p. 34 – 38.

(41) See Bèze, *Correspondance,* I, p. 201 – 202 and Davis, 'Peletier and Beza part company', p. 214 – 215. According to Jugé, who seems not to have discerned allusions to Peletier in the preface to *Abraham,* 'De Bèze garde le silence sur Peletier' (p. 83).

(42) See his *Œuvres poetiques,* facsimile reproduction of the Paris, 1547 edition by M. Françon (Rochecorbon, 1958),

p. 209 – 217. The poems are also in the edition by L. Séché and P. Laumonier, Paris, 1904, p. 74 – 79.

(43) See Bèze's *Correspondance,* I, p. 202, n. 10.

(44) According to Natalie Davis, Peletier included in the first edition of his *Aritmetique* (February 1550) four dedicatory proems to Bèze; and he presented Bèze and their joint friends as speakers in his *Dialogue de l'Ortografe* of January 1551. Peletier included in his *Ortografe* a paragraph (dating from late 1548 or early 1549) stating he did not know why Bèze had left France, and gave a verdict on Bèze's poems (p. 48 – 49). He retained dedicatory proems to Bèze in the second edition of his *Aritmetique* in 1552. In 1554, the third edition appeared, with all mention of Bèze suppressed. Nothing is known of any relationship between Peletier and Bèze beyond this date. See 'Peletier and Beza part company', p. 188 – 189. The preface to *Abraham sacrifiant* is dated 1 October 1550, so the *Ortografe* may have gone to press before Peletier knew Bèze had attacked him (for editions of *Abraham,* see F. Gardy, *Bibliographie des œuvres théologiques, littéraires, historiques et juridiques de Théodore de Bèze,* Genève, 1960, nos. 23 – 50).

(45) A friend of his, Estienne Pasquier, recalled that 'Au paravant qu'il [Bèze] eust changé de religion, il avoit pour compaignon Jacques Peletier'; see *Les Recherches de la France,* VI, vii; p. 738 in the Paris, 1611 edition (B.L. 596 g 4).

(46) Perhaps he was influenced by Calvin: see my 'Théodore de Bèze and Philænus', *Bibliothèque d'Humanisme et Renaissance,* LII, 1990, p. 352 – 353.

(47) A. Bernus, *Théodore de Bèze à Lausanne,* Lausanne, 1900, p. 40 – 41.

(48) On Bèze's work as a translator of the psalms, see P.F. Geisendorf, *Théodore de Bèze,* Genève, 1949, p. 54 – 63; on the Reformers' psalm translations generally, see P. Pidoux, *Le Psautier huguenot du XVIe siècle,* 2 v., Bâle, 1962.

(49) See M. Jeanneret, 'Marot traducteur des Psaumes entre le néo-platonisme et la Réforme', *Bibliothèque d'Humanisme et Renaissance,* XXVII, 1965, p. 629–643.

(50) See Théodore de Bèze, *Psaumes mis en vers français (1551–1562), accompagnés de la version en prose de Loïs Budé,* ed. P. Pidoux, Genève, 1984. For a facsimile of one of the many 1562 editions (by Michel Blanchier, Geneva), see C. Marot, T. de Bèze, *Les psaumes en vers français avec leurs mélodies,* ed. P. Pidoux (T.L.F.), Genève, 1986.

(51) Some of the theological resonance of *L'Olive* has however been pointed out. See G. Gadoffre, *Du Bellay et le sacré,* Paris, 1978, I, 'Amour sacré et amour profane', p. 17–44, and the notes in Ernesta Caldarini's edition of the poems, Genève, 1981.

(52) He invoked the example of Martial: 'Parcere personis, dicere de vitiis': see my *Joachim Du Bellay's Veiled Victim,* Genève, 1974, p. 3–5, 11.

(53) The translation, made between 1540 and 1548, enjoyed vast popularity in France, especially at the court: 'Jamais livre ne fut embrassé avecq' tant de faveur que cestuy, l'espace de vingt ans ou environ', wrote Estienne Pasquier (cited, from *Recherches de la France,* VI, 5, by H. Chamard in *Joachim Du Bellay, 1522–1560,* Lille, 1900, p. 264). Ronsard had read the novel and some of his poems are inspired by it: see Laumonier, *Ronsard poète lyrique,* 2ᵉ éd., Paris, 1923, p. 221. Laumonier recalled there that translations of *Amadis* by Herberay Des Essars, Claude Colet, Jacques Gohorry and Guillaume Aubert appeared between 1540 and 1566, and that Books IX–XII of the *Amadis,* published between 1552 and 1556, contain preliminary verses by Dorat, Du Bellay, Baïf, Jodelle, Magny, Jean-Pierre de Mesmes, Muret, Belleau, Tahureau and Pasquier. But the popularity of the work was to wane: see M. Simonin, 'La disgrâce d'Amadis', *Studi francesi,* LXXXII, 1984, p. 1–35.

(54) From an *Ode au Seigneur Des Essars sur le discours de son Amadis,* in the *Monomachie de David et de Goliath,* ed. E. Caldarini, Genève, 1981, p. 123 – 126. Bèze attacked translations of Amadis in the 1569 edition of his *Poemata* (*Correspondance,* X, p. 92); the passage is cited later in this book.

(55) The pretext for the insinuation was an epigram in the *Poemata* in which Bèze, returning from a journey, debates whether to embrace first his Candida or his fellow-scholar Germain Audebert (see his *Correspondance,* X, p. 97, n. 18). Audebert was extolled also by Du Bellay (S.T.F.M., V, p. 272).

(56) See Cicero, *De natura Deorum,* I, i, (2), etc., and a poem titled *Petri Ronsardi responsum* (probably by Jean Dorat, its title notwithstanding), published with Ronsard's *Responce aux injures* (p. 213 – 214 in my edition of his *Discours des miseres*).

(57) The sonnet against Du Bellay and his replies are in Du Bellay, S.T.F.M., II, p. 206 – 210.

(58) Ronsard, S.T.F.M., III, p. 145 – 146.

(59) Ronsard, S.T.F.M., VIII, p. 357.

(60) From Bèze, *Correspondance,* I, p. 210 – 211; the probable date of composition of the poem is 1551. It appeared in editions of the *Psaumes* in 1553 and later (see the editors' note, p. 207). On Ronsard's practice of referring to kings as 'gods', see my 'Opium of the people: Numa Pompilius in the French Renaissance', *Bibliothèque d'Humanisme et Renaissance,* LII, 1990, p. 12 – 16.

(61) See *2 Corinthians,* XI, 12 – 15 and the note in my edition of Ronsard's *Discours des miseres,* p. 134.

(62) On the possibility that he saw the play performed, see his *Œuvres complètes,* ed. E. Balmas, 2 v., Paris, 1965, 1968, II, p. 435 – 436. We know from one of the sonnets he later wrote against the ministers of the Reformed faith that Jodelle spent some time in Geneva: see Balmas's edition, I, p. 281 and 504. Simon Goulart also informs us of this: 'Estienne

Jodelle Parisien [...] a autresfois demeuré à Geneve, faisant profession de la Religion, où il fit en une nuict entre autres cent vers latins, esquels il deschiroit la messe avec des brocards convenables' (cited, from his *Memoires de l'estat de France,* 1579, I, 278*vo*, by H. Chamard in *Histoire de la Pléiade,* 4 v., Paris, 1939 – 1940, III, p. 209, n. 1).

(63) See Balmas's edition, I, p. 37 and (for the text) 263.

(64) See Balmas's edition, I, p. 495 – 496, where the editor discusses the little that remains of the poetry Jodelle wrote in favour of the Reformed faith.

(65) From Balmas's edition, I, p. 263 – 264.

(66) Quoted from M. Raymond, *L'Influence de Ronsard sur la poésie française (1550 – 1585),* nouv. éd., Genève, 1965, I, p. 335.

(67) See notably his 37 sonnets *Contre les ministres de la nouvelle opinion* (Balmas's edition, I, p. 267 – 285).

(68) One of his sonnets against the Reformed ministers declares that he would weep with them when one of their number is burned for his opinions — were it not that they themselves argue in favour of the burning of all heretics: possibly (as Balmas observed) an allusion to Bèze's *De haereticis a civili magistratu puniendis.* See Balmas's edition, I, p. 281 – 282 and 504.

(69) Contemporary testimony on Jodelle's atheism comes from Simon Goulart, Innocent Gentillet and Pierre de L'Estoile (and, according to the latter, Ronsard). See Chamard, *Histoire de la Pléiade,* III, p. 209 – 211 and, for L'Estoile, his *Registre-Journal du règne de Henri III,* ed. M. Lazard and G. Schrenck, Genève, 1992, p. 109, 149 – 151. A curious poem by Florent Chrestien about a copy of Jodelle's *Didon* being devoured by dogs seems to me to contain, in its conclusion, a reference to Jodelle's atheism (text in P. de Nolhac, *Ronsard et l'humanisme,* Paris, 1966, p. 188, n. 2). Jodelle died abandoned by his friends; conceivably (as Chamard suggested), his

rejection of both religions had something to do with this, for it could be dangerous to consort with known atheists.

(70) He subsequently taught philosophy in Geneva, where he died in October 1560. Bèze dedicated a poem to him in the undated [1588?] edition of his *Poemata,* and included in this edition a poem by Tagaut titled *Philomela*; he also included in this work an epitaph of Tagaut. See Gardy, *Bibliographie des œuvres de Théodore de Bèze,* no. 8. On Tagaut and Bèze, see the latter's *Correspondance,* I, p. 61 – 62, 183 – 184. On Tagaut, see also M. Raymond, 'Jean Tagaut, poète français et bourgeois de Genève', *Revue du seizième siècle,* 1925.

(71) See J. Pineaux, *La Poésie des Protestants de langue française,* Paris, 1971, p. 45.

(72) Quoted by M. Raymond in *L'Influence de Ronsard sur la poésie française (1550 – 1585),* nouv. éd., Genève, 1965, I, p. 341 – 342.

(73) Quoted from Raymond, *L'Influence de Ronsard,* I, p. 333.

(74) Raymond included Babinot among Catholic poets (I, p. 329) apparently on the strength of the following statement by Babinot: 'Suis-je heretique, ennemi de la Foi? / Non, mais je suis catholiq...'; but sixteenth-century writers who described themselves as 'catholique' were not always being very specific — you could reject papal supremacy and retain creeds which endorse the 'catholic and apostolic church'. On Babinot's conversion by Calvin, see N. W[eiss], 'La Christiade d'Albert Babinot', *Bulletin de la Société de l'Histoire du Protestantisme français,* XXXVII, 1888, p. 112.

(75) See Pineaux, *Poésie des Protestants,* p. 262 – 263 (I have reproduced the text as given there by Pineaux), and J. Vignes, 'Paraphrase et appropriation: les avatars poétiques de l'*Ecclésiaste* au temps des guerres de religion (Dalbiac, Carle, Belleau, Baïf)', *Bibliothèque d'Humanisme et Renaissance,* LV, 1993, p. 521. According to Vignes (p. 506), Dalbiac was mur-

dered in Tours in 1562 for refusing to abjure his Reformed convictions.

(76) See D. Boccassini, *La parola riscritta,* Firenze, 1985, especially p. 60 – 67, and E. Balmas, 'Guillaume Guéroult traducteur des « Psaumes »', *Revue d'Histoire littéraire de la France,* LXVII, 1967, p. 705 – 725.

(77) Davis states that Peletier 'contributed several essays' to this work, though without saying which ones. Her grounds: (a) the Marnefs obtained the *privilegium* for the work on 7 March 1547 (i.e., 1548), the same date as the *privilegia* for the *Orthography* and the *Arithmetic*; (b) some of the orthography is distinctly Peletier's, e.g. *Meilheure, oreilhes, ailheurs, terroer* (p. 20), *ans, blans* (p. 50); *grammariens* (p. 18); (c) there is a similarity of themes between many of the essays and Peletier's concerns at that period ('Peletier and Beza part company', p. 197, n. 39). A. Chenevière showed that chapter XX comes from Elie Vinet's works and suggested other chapters written by him (*Bonaventure des Périers,* Paris, 1886, pp. 245 – 246). Jugé ascribed certain chapters (V, VIII, XII, XVII, XVIII and XXI) with varying degrees of probability to Peletier (see *Jacques Peletier du Mans,* Paris, 1907, pp. 322 – 325). G.-A. Pérouse, who discusses the text in *Nouvelles françaises du XVIᵉ siècle* (Genève, 1977, p. 178 – 184) hints, but on no better grounds than its links with Poitiers, that Jacques Tahureau may have had a hand in it (p. 181). It has sometimes been suggested that Jean Bonaventure Des Périers had a hand in it, but the suggestion was rejected by L. Sozzi in *Les Contes de Bonaventure des Périers,* Torino, 1965, p. 48.

(78) I have used the copy in the British Library (Hirsch, I, 593). The passage I have cited is on p. 66.

(79) The motto 'la mort ni [i.e. n'y] mort' is found in works by Marot: see for example C.A. Mayer, *Bibliographie des œuvres de Clément Marot, II, Editions,* Genève, 1954, p. 22, nos. 25, 26, 27.

(80) Jugé argued that it could not be by Peletier: 'Comment, dans ce recueil anonyme de 1547, Peletier tournerait-il en dérision le mot « ode », qu'il écrit avec respect dans les œuvres de la même année?' (p. 323). But (i) Jugé was mistaken on the date, which is 1548 new style, and (ii) it is not the word 'ode' that the author derides. However, there is a different (and in my view compelling) reason why Peletier is most unlikely to have written the chapter: we know he offered encouragement to Ronsard early in the latter's career, and he also has positive remarks in the *Art poëtique* of 1555 about Ronsard's *Odes*.

(81) As well as endorsing Marot's psalm translations, Bèze had defended Marot in 1537 against Sagon: see Bèze's *In Maromastigas,* published by F. Aubert, J. Boussard and H. Meylan in 'Un premier recueil de poésies latines de Théodore de Bèze', *Bibliothèque d'Humanisme et Renaissance,* XV, 1953 p. 178 (and see p. 291 for two Latin adaptations, possibly by Bèze, of French poems by Marot). Bèze also praised Marot in his *Poemata* of 1548 (p. 67).

(82) Quoted from I. Silver, *The intellectual evolution of Ronsard, I, The formative influences,* St. Louis, 1969, p. 165.

(83) See Raymond, *Influence de Ronsard,* I, p. 335 and (especially) M.A. Harris, *A study of Théodose Valentinian's 'Amant resuscité de la mort d'amour',* Genève, 1966.

(84) See Raymond I, p. 335–336. The previous year, in an oration *De dignitate ac præstantia studii theologii,* Muret had stressed the preeminence of King David as a poet, and his superiority to Orpheus, Homer and Pindar. See Demerson, *Mythologie classique,* p. 256.

(85) *Chansons tressalutaires et catholiques pour les bons chrestiens, à l'honneur de Dieu et de nostre mere saincte Eglise,* Rouen, 1554, B.L. 11475 a 8, verso of A ii^{ro}, A iii^{ro}, verso of titlepage, 21vo.

(86) See A.J. Steele, 'Conversions', *Cahiers de l'Association internationale des études françaises,* X, 1958, p. 69–88.

(87) In the *Servitude volontaire,* La Boëtie deplores the fact that French kings have sought to 'accoustumer le peuple envers eus, non seulement à obeissance et servitude, mais ancore à devotion' (p. 65 in my edition, Genève, 1967) — thereby attacking precisely that language of divinity which Ronsard applied to the sovereign, notably in the odes. La Boëtie's *In adulatores poetas* is in his *Œuvres complètes,* ed. L. Desgraves, 2v., Bordeaux, 1991, II, p. 66 – 67.

(88) *Les Lettres,* Paris, 1586, B.L. 636 i 21, 14ro. The letter can also be found E. Pasquier, *Choix de lettres sur la littérature, la langue et la traduction,* ed. D. Thickett, Genève, 1956, p. 4 – 8

(89) On this, see especially A. Gordon, *Ronsard et la rhétorique,* Genève, 1970, p. 49 – 72; also the studies cited in my 'Ronsard et ses critiques contemporains', p. 85, n. 12.

(90) In his *Ad Claudium Espencium, nobilissimum et doctissimum theologum, de poesi Christiana judicium et exemplum*:

> Qui, pater ESPENCI, qui fit res carmine sacras
> Ut pauci tractent hodie, vix unus et alter,
> Vatibus innumeris quum regia perstrepat aula?
> An genus hoc hominum nullus (Epicurus ut olim)
> Autumnat esse Deos, et rident sacra profani?
> An duram et sterilem fugiunt, neque versibus aptam
> Materiem, in qua vix florens et nobile sese
> Jactare ingenium, famamque advivere possit?...

From his *Œuvres complètes,* ed. P.J.S. Duféy, 3t., Paris, 1824 – 25, III, p. 41.

(91) See M. Raymond, 'Deux pamphlets inconnus contre Ronsard et la Pléiade', *Revue du seizième siècle,* XIII, 1926, p. 243 – 264; he noted that the *privilegium* of Macer's book is dated 8 July 1555 (p. 245, n. 2).

(92) The document was published by Raymond in 'Deux pamphlets inconnus'. His remarks about Bèze and Geneva leave little room for doubt about Rivaudeau's religious sympathies. But according to Pineaux, he was a Reformer: see 'De Ronsard

à Ovide: un humaniste protestant devant la poésie d'amour'
Bulletin de la Société de l'Histoire du Protestantisme Français,
CXXVII, 1982, p. 477–492.

(93) See his *Œuvres poétiques,* ed. C. Nourain de Sourdeval,
Paris, 1859, p. 223–226 (an *Epistre à Remy Belleau poëte*
which attacks critics of Ronsard) and p. 232–233 (a passage
in an *Epistre à Babinot poëte chrestien*). One of the 1563
pamphlets against Ronsard, an anonymous *Remonstrance à la
Royne,* has been attributed by Pineaux to Rivaudeau (see his
Polémique protestante contre Ronsard, Paris, 1973, p. 99–102).
Rivaudeau does not appear to allude to Ronsard in his *Aman,
tragedie saincte,* published in his *Œuvres* of 1566 (see the edition by K. Cameron: Genève, Paris, 1969).

(94) Du Bellay, S.T.F.M., IV, p. 116.

(95) Du Bellay, S.T.F.M., IV, p. 129.

(96) Du Bellay, S.T.F.M., IV, p. 137–138.

(97) Du Bellay, S.T.F.M., IV, p. 147.

(98) On the contemporary reaction, see Laumonier, *Ronsard
poète lyrique,* 2e éd., Paris, 1923, p. 103–105. Laumonier
observed however that these poems appealed to Baïf, Muret,
Tahureau and Magny.

(99) Ronsard, S.T.F.M., VIII, p. 207–208.

(100) 'Ronsard, toujours docile à la voix de l'amitié, commença
tout de suite (nous le savons par P. Des Mireurs, qui l'avait
sans doute appris de Morel) son *Hymne de l'Hercule Chrestien,*
pour racheter l'excessive liberté des *Folastries*' (Laumonier,
Ronsard poète lyrique, p. 105).

(101) On Christian use of the Hercules legends, see Ronsard,
S.T.F.M., VIII, p. 223, n. 1; M. Simon, *Hercule et le christianisme,* Paris, 1955, p. 167–191; and especially M.R. Jung,
Hercule dans la littérature française du XVIe siècle, Genève,
1960, p. 105–125.

(102) Nicolas Denisot extolled the poem in a sonnet published with it (see Ronsard, S.T.F.M., VIII, p. 206). Early defenders of the poem include Colletet and Besly (see S.T.F.M., VIII, p. xxv and 223, n. 1); see also Jung, *Hercule*, p. 119 – 121.

(103) On hostility of Reformers, see Jung, *Hercule*, p. 121 – 122. But Ronsard's poem also had Catholic critics: see Jung, p. 122 – 123 (Gabrielle de Coignard and La Boderie), and Ronsard, S.T.F.M., revised edition by R. Lebègue, 1963, VIII, p. 373.

(104) See Ronsard, S.T.F.M., VII, p. 115. On the date of the collection, see S.T.F.M., VII, p. xx – xxi.

(105) See Ronsard, S.T.F.M., VII, 229 – 230.

(106) See Ronsard. S.T.F.M., VII, p. 315 – 316.

(107) See Ronsard. S.T.F.M., VIII, p. 69. The argument has been used by monotheists of any persuasion who wished to 'exonerate' writings by polytheists. It is found, notably, in Cicero's *De natura deorum* (II, xxviii, 71): 'deus pertinens per naturam cuiusque rei, per terras Ceres, per maria Neptunus, alii per alia, poterunt intellegi qui qualesque sint quoque eos nomine consuetudo nuncupaverit'; see also the notes at this point in the edition by A.S. Pease, 2 v., Cambridge, Mass., 1953, 1958. See also D.P. Walker, 'Orpheus the theologian', in his *The Ancient Theology*, London, 1972, p. 22 – 41 (on Proclus, Pletho, Ficino, Walter Raleigh and Lefèvre de La Boderie). In a preface to his *Franciade*, Ronsard wrote of 'Dieu, auquel les hommes attribuent autant de noms qu'il a de puissances et de vertus' (see S.T.F.M., XVI, p. 345).

(108) See Ronsard, S.T.F.M., VIII, p. 100. According to Laumonier, the passage was inspired by Lucretius. Ronsard several times depicts underworld torments as representations of remorse: see I. Silver, 'Ronsard's ethical thought', *Bibliothèque d'Humanisme et Renaissance*, XXIV, 1962, p. 89 – 92.

(109) See Ronsard. S.T.F.M., VIII, p. 291 – 292. Ronsard elsewhere equates the Harpies and flatterers: see Ronsard,

S.T.F.M., X, p. 297 and XI, p. 85 (*Remonstrance au peuple,* l. 415 – 420).

(110) This is a large and relatively untouched subject. Some passages which, given the intellectual habits of the age, lend themselves to a syncretist interpretation are (in the S.T.F.M. edition): II, p. 111 – 112 (cf. 182; parallel between Prometheus and Adam); II, p. 172 (echo of Horace and of *Matthew* VI, 8, cf. 31 – 32); III, p. 144 – 145 (waters of Helicon and baptism); and see Maddison, *Apollo and the Nine,* p. 234.

(111) It seems that the Reformation and the Council of Trent led to a more severe attitude towards mythology on the part of all Christians (see Walker, *Ancient Theology,* p. 31 – 33). But in the case of Catholics, official severity seems simply to have heightened attempts to disculpate mythology by allegorical interpretations: see J. Seznec, *The Survival of the Pagan Gods,* New York, 1953, p. 263 – 278.

(112) See Ronsard, S.T.F.M., IX, p. 157 – 158. The simile of the potter, used to show that God's grace is conferred in accordance with his inscrutable will, is in *Romans,* IX, 20 – 24.

(113) Parisiis, B.L. C 39 f 24 (2), p. 2.

(114) S.l., s.d., B. Nat. Ye 2433, B v^{ro}.

(115) In La Boëtie's *Œuvres complètes,* ed. L. Desgraves, 2 v., Bordeaux, 1991, II, p. 65. Another adversary of love poetry was the author, one 'D.V.' (De Villemadon?) who, in a letter dated 26 August 1559 and addressed to the Queen Mother, denounced the Cardinal of Lorraine for deflecting her from the psalm translations of Marot and propagating the 'infâmes amours' of certain 'beaux poëtes du diable' who engulf their readers 'en abysme de toute iniquité et désordre, voire de toute impieté' (see V.-L. Saulnier, 'Autour de la lettre dite de Ville-madon', *Bibliothèque d'Humanisme et Renaissance,* XXXVIII, 1975, p. 349 – 376; the text of the letter is in the *Mémoires de Condé,* 6v., London, 1743, I, p. 620 – 629). According to Laumonier (Ronsard, S.T.F.M., X, p. 364, n. 6), Ronsard was

also reproached for his love poetry by Jérome L'Huillier, but Laumonier did not quote his source for this.

(116) The letter is in Bèze's *Correspondance*, III, p. 42 – 52.

(117) As we know from his famous letter to Jean Du Bellay in defence of these poems: see Y. Bellenger, *Du Bellay, ses «Regrets» qu'il fit dans Rome*, Paris, 1975, p. 430 – 431.

(118) *L'Hospital*, besides being the dedicatee of the famous *Ode* of 1553 (see Ronsard, S.T.F.M. III, 118 – 163), was extolled subsequently by Ronsard: see S.T.F.M., VI, 82; IX, 68, 70, 84, 87 – 88; XIII, 29 ('le docte Hospital immortel de renom') and 157. *Monluc:* see S.T.F.M., XII, 182 – 183 (the passage extols Monluc as an almost unique example of a good bishop); XIII, 245 – 246, 261 (see variant title of the poem); XVIII, 510 – 511. *Foix:* see S.T.F.M., XIII, 150 – 158.

(119) See my edition of the *Discours des miseres*, p. 27 – 29 and the note on p. 28; he also counselled 'douceur' later (see Ronsard, S.T.F.M., XVII, p. 26).

(120) See the *Elegie à Des Autels*, l. 77 – 112; *Remonstrance au peuple*, l. 367 – 450; *Responce aux injures*, l. 437 – 462 (p. 33 – 34, 123 – 127 and 176 – 177 respectively in my edition of the *Discours*).

(121) He extolled Odet de Coligny (Cardinal Chastillon) and François Peroceli (or Perussel), chaplain of Louis de Condé (see my edition of the *Discours des miseres*, p. 97 and note and 89 – 90 and note).

(122) He rejoiced that after the first civil war, 'Morts sont ces motz Papaux et Huguenotz' (S.T.F.M., XIII, p. 149); and he gave a courtier the advice, 'Ne romps ton tranquille repos / Pour Papaux ne pour Huguenotz' (S.T.F.M., XIII, p. 260). Both poems were published in 1565, in the *Elegies, Mascarades et Bergerie*.

(123) As he put it in the *Remonstrance au peuple de France* (line 458 in the original edition). The sentiment is typical of

Ronsard: see p. 22–23 of my edition of the *Discours des miseres* (Genève, 1979).

(124) See S.T.F.M., XI, p. 101, n. 2; XVIII, 298 and note; 321–324.

(125) 'J'euz amy en ce temps le divin Pelletier', wrote Des Masures in his elegy to Ronsard discussed below (referring to the time before his, Des Masures's, exile from France; Ronsard, S.T.F.M., X, p. 149). 'Peletier praised his [Des Masures's] work in the *Art poetique*, p. 13' — Davis, 'Peletier and Beza part company', p. 218, n. 116, referring to the Lyons, 1555 edition of the *Art poetique*.

(126) Laumonier remarked (S.T.F.M., X, p. 145, n. 1) that Des Masures was exiled from France on the order of the King 'pour intelligence avec l'ennemi allemand'. Michel Simonin suggested the grounds were his religious opinions ('Les relations de Des Masures avec Dorat et Ronsard', *Bulletin du Bibliophile*, 1, 1990, p. 77 and 82), but this seems on the whole unlikely since in 1550, and again in 1554, Bèze was urging him to adopt the Reformed faith; and when, in the late 1550s, he organized a Reformed Church in Lorraine, he did so at first surreptitiously.

(127) See M. Chopard, 'Louis Des Masures en Lorraine: une source de l'*Histoire de martyrs* de Crespin', *Mélanges V.L. Saulnier,* ed. P.G. Castex, Genève, 1984 p. 630.

(128) See Bèze's *Correspondance,* I, p. 61–62.

(129) See *Correspondance,* I, p. 146. After referring to Des Masures's sickness, Bèze wrote: 'Je le prie d'avoir souvenance de mon affaire par ses amys de par dela, s'il s'offre quelque bonne occasion. Car peult estre que Nostre Seigneur luy aura touché le cueur en sa necessité'. For the editors, this 'affaire' is the issue of Des Masures's share in the task of translating the psalms, but given the content of the earlier letter (which relates Bèze's encouragement to Des Masures to adopt the Reformed faith) and the remark here about God touching his heart in his

hour of need, the 'affaire' to which Bèze refers seems to be Des Masures's conversion.

(130) See Bèze's *Correspondance,* X, p. 286, n. 1, where the text of Bèze's poem is given (it was to be included in the 1569 edition of Bèze's *Poemata,* as well as in Des Masures's *De Babylonis ruina,* also published in 1569). According to Gardy, an undated [1588?] edition of Bèze's poems contains this poem, followed by (p. 41–47) *Eiusdem Ludovici Masurii ad Theodorum Bezam epistola,* and (p. 48–50) *Eiusdem Masurii canticum Mosis* (*Bibliographie des œuvres de Bèze,* no. 8); and a 1590 edition of Bèze's Latin verse translation of the psalms contains Latin poetry by Des Masures (Gardy, no. 235).

(131) For the text, see Chopard, 'Louis Des Masures en Lorraine', p. 634–638.

(132) The following is a sample:

> [...] De ce bien comparable à nul autre bonheur,
> Par toy m'a l'Eternel esté large donneur;
> Pour ce bien me donner de grace pure et pleine,
> Il t'a mis en besongne et a choisi ta peine.
> Tu m'as, comme il a pleu au Seigneur te dresser,
> Esveillé du sommeil; tu m'es venu presser,
> Si qu'en moy lent et froid, par ta soigneuse presse,
> S'est duite et convertie à l'œuvre ma paresse.
> O comme de bon cœur et de fidele voix,
> Sur le bord sablonneux du beau lac Genevois,
> Un jour (dont à jamais il me souviendra), comme
> Passant je retournois du conclave de Romme,
> Tu m'enhortas de suivre et fermement tenir
> La verité certaine [...]

Quoted from Bèze's *Correspondance,* VI, p. 315 (which reproduces the text from Des Masures's *Vingtsix cantiques chantés au Seigneur,* Lyon, 1564). Des Masures goes on to summarize exhortations in the 'lettres tant exquises' which Bèze sent him (which are lost).

(133) The relevant part of the poem, which is titled *Eiusdem Ludovici Masurii ad Theodorum Bezam Epistola*, is the beginning:

> Consilium a veteri petis et solamen amico,
> Rebus ut in duris animum obfirmare, novosque
> Cor quibus afficitur valeas perferre dolores.
> Ast ipsum potius te nos, ubi dura premit sors,
> Consulimus: tu das animos imbellibus acres.
> Nimirum te Beza suum Pater æquus alumnum
> Viribus ingenii validis instruxit, iniquos
> Fortis ut invicto contemnas pectore casus,
> Utque tuis, ne sæva pios vis auferat, adsis,
> Tu sociis, et voce iuves, et viribus instes.
> Tene viam certæ primum hortatore salutis
> Corripui, loca senta situ qui cæcus obibam?
> Tune mihi authorem vitæ, pede pallida tristi
> Irrueret ne mors, et metam falce se caret,
> Monstrasti, recto sequeret quem tramite Christum?

Bèze, *Poemata*, 1569 (B.L. 1213 1 5), in a section titled *Carmina quæ ad eius poemata antea excusa accesserunt*, p. 41 – 42. The poem follows Bèze's eulogy of Des Masures's *Babylone*. It is followed (p. 48) by Des Masures's Latin paraphrase of the Canticle of Moses (from *Exodus*, XV). Des Masures's poem in praise of Bèze is also in Bèze's *Correspondance*, X, p. 281 – 286.

(134) Pineaux, *Poésie des Protestants*, p. 459 – 460.

(135) Bèze's text had been first published in 1561: see Gardy, *Bibliographie des œuvres de Théodore de Bèze*, no. 137 and Bèze's *Correspondance*, III, p. 84, n. 1 and 97, n. 2. Des Masures's translation appeared in 1564 (Lyon, Jan d'Ogerolles, in-12) with the title *Bref traitté des sacremens en general* (see *Histoire ecclesiastique des Eglises Réformées de France*, ed. G. Baum, E. Cunitz, 3 t., Paris, 1883 – 89, III, p. 565, n. 1).

(136) I reproduced his repudiation of his pagan poetry (from his *Œuvres poetiques*, Lion, 1557, B.N. Rés., Ye 366, p. 43) in 'Ronsard et ses critiques contemporains', p. 87. Du Bellay's

praise of his translation of the *Aeneid* is in the dedicatory letter to Jean de Morel in his *Quatriesme livre de l'Eneide de Virgile,* of 1552 (S.T.F.M., VI, p. 250) and in *Les Regrets,* s. 148.

(137) *Vingt pseaumes de David traduits selon la verité hebraïque et mis en rime françoise,* Lyon. Apparently, this translation of the psalms was undertaken at the behest of the Cardinal of Lorraine (doubtless Jean). But Des Masures avoided translating psalms previously translated by Bèze (with two exceptions), so the work may have as its genesis the urgings of the Reformer in 1550. See Chopard, 'Louis Des Masures en Lorraine', p. 631.

(138) See his *Tragédies saintes: David combattant, David triomphant, David fugitif,* ed. C. Comte, Paris, 1907, p. 9, 97. On the Geneva edition, see Chopard, p. 633 (and notes), 637.

(139) 'Cunctantemque metu et rerum telluris amantem': quoted, from *Ad Claudium filium adulescentem,* in the *Poemata* of 1574, by Pineaux, *Poésie des Protestants,* p. 255.

(140) See the comments of Pineaux, *La Poésie des Protestants,* p. 253 – 255.

(141) As we know from *Ad Claudium filium adolescentem.* On these events, see Pineaux, *Poésie des Protestants,* p. 460 and Chopard, 'Louis Des Masures en Lorraine', p. 631 – 633 and notes.

(142) He was the 'chef spirituel' of this community from 1558 to the end of 1561: see Pineaux, *Poésie des Protestants,* p. 461. According to A. Cullière (in a review of *Ronsard et la Rome protestante,* in *Bibliothèque d'Humanisme et Renaissance,* XLVIII, 1986, p. 282), Des Masures never became a pastor in the Reformed Church.

(143) See Chopard, 'Louis Des Masures en Lorraine', p. 632.

(144) See S.T.F.M., X, p. 145 – 160.

(145) See Pineaux, *Poésie des Protestants,* p. 21 – 22.

(146) 'On conçoit bien comment Bèze continuait d'espérer convertir à la nouvelle religion le prince des poètes qu'il avait croisé jadis à Paris. Est-il aventuré de penser qu'il aurait fait savoir à Des Masures, mieux placé que quiconque en raison de l'amitié que lui marquait publiquement Ronsard, qu'il se devait de s'employer à le convaincre?' (Simonin, 'Les relations de Des Masures', p. 84).

(147) See Ronsard, S.T.F.M., X, p. 162 – 163.

(148) On the date of the collection, see the *Advertissement au lecteur* which precedes it (S.T.F.M., X, p. 3).

(149) My source for the relationship between Des Masures and Melissus, and the latter and Ronsard, is P. de Nolhac, *Un Poète rhénan ami de la Pléiade, Paul Melissus,* Paris, 1923. According to Nolhac (p. 8), 'Leurs recueils poétiques [*sc.* those of Des Masures and Melissus] se rempliront de leurs confidences réciproques', and he refers to Melissus's *Schediasmata* of 1574, p. 177 and the 1575 edition of the same work, p. 364. He noted that the Latin translation of Ronsard's sonnet is in the 1574 edition, p. 43. On Bèze's praise of Melissus, see p. 94 (and cf. Gardy, *Bibliographie des œuvres de Bèze,* nos. 5, 6, 11, 229). Melissus met Ronsard in Paris 1567; Nolhac presented (*passim*) the copious evidence for his admiration for the poet.

(150) The *Elegie à Guillaume Des Autels* was later included by Ronsard in editions of his complete works among the *Discours des miseres* (p. 27 – 41 in my edition of the *Discours,* Genève, 1979). The poems included in the 1560 edition of Ronsard's *Œuvres* are in S.T.F.M., X.

(151) The *Elegie à Loïs Des Masures* is in Ronsard, S.T.F.M., X (p. 362 – 370) and in my edition of the *Discours des miseres* (Genève, 1979, p. 43 – 50).

(152) See P. Laumonier, *Ronsard poète lyrique, 2e éd.,* Paris, 1923, p. 82 – 83. Laumonier surmises there that La Haye had helped Joachim Du Bellay make his peace with Thomas Sebillet after attacking him in the *Deffence et illustration* of 1549. Du

Bellay's poem in praise of La Haye, titled *Au seigneur Robert de La Haye pour estrene*, appeared in the *Œuvres de l'invention de l'autheur*, published with the *Quatriesme livre de l'Eneide* (see Du Bellay, S.T.F.M., IV, p. 178 – 182; Du Bellay also composed an *Estrene* for La Haye's sister Marie, who had written an ode in praise of Du Bellay and Ronsard — S.T.F.M., IV, p. 182 – 184). Ronsard's early poem in praise of La Haye is the *Contr'estrene, au seigneur Robert de La Haye*, published in the *Cinquiesme livre des odes* of 1552 (see Ronsard, S.T.F.M., III, p. 164 – 170).

(153) See Laumonier, *Ronsard poète lyrique*, 2e éd., p. 105, n. 2, referring to his article in *Revue de la Renaissance*, 1902, p. 3 and 4.

(154) La Haye's poem is in Ronsard, S.T.F.M., VII, p. 111 – 112; Ronsard's paraphrase is in S.T.F.M., X, p. 307 (at the end of the *Elegie* dedicated to Pierre L'Escot).

(155) S.T.F.M., X, p. 320 – 321.

(156) There is a facsimile of the text in J.P. Barbier, *Ma bibliothèque poétique, II, Ronsard*, Genève, 1990, p. 339, and I have based the following transcription upon it:

Qui populos legum sacro rexere superbos
Imperio quondam atque animos domuere feroces
Quique suas sanctis auxerunt moribus urbes,
Saepe suos procul exterres fecere poetas:
Nempe solent rari sinuoso tramite et æstu
Per maria et scopulos, et tot discrimina, veræ
Virtutis sacros infossi ambire recessus,
Quum sua tegminibus pars mulcet pectora opacis,
Soliciti tantum latas explere lacunas
Latrantis stomachi, ast ad cætera munia prorsus
Ignavi et nimium fragiles operumque perosi
Et soliti exemplis operosos frangere cives.
Ecce redit prisca, qualis sub consule forma
Roma vetus, redeunt censores, et venerandæ
Sacrarum legum tabulæ, redit ipse Licurgus:
CAROLUS, æthereo missus de sidere nimbo,

Aurea virtutis divinæ secla reducit,
Purgat et errorem pelagus populosque reformat.
Dejicite exuvias nudum nomenque poetæ,
Et si qua est pietas animis, si restat et ulla
Religio, summum dociles audite sonantem,
Invisi qui sunt vani, et qui vana loquuntur,
Quosque superstitio fictorum falsa deorum
Raptat et æterni rapientes patris honores,
In quos extensa vibrat sua fulmina dextra:
Aut si nulla tenet vestrum reverentia pectus
Numinis, este tamen, vestra vel vindice Musa
Et patriæ et vobis vestrisque parentibus æqui.

Bèze obtained the permission for publication of the psalms by Antoine Vincent on 19 October 1561: see his *Correspondance,* III, p. 144 and 145, n. 17; 175, n. 13. On Chrestien, see F. Vian, 'Florent Chrestien lecteur et traducteur d'Apollonios de Rhodes', *Bibliothèque d'Humanisme et Renaissance,* XXXIV, 1972, p. 471 – 482.

(157) See Bèze's *Correspondance,* IV, p. 295 – 296. The editors observe that the dedication of Courcelles's *Cantique des Cantiques* to Condé is dated 15 January 1561 in Paris (which almost certainly means 1562 n.s., for Bèze was in Paris in January 1562).

(158) Text taken from Pineaux, *Poésie des Protestants,* p. 247.

(159) The poem is in my edition of the *Discours,* p. 149 – 215, and the passage cited here is on p. 204. On the large number of early editions of the text, see my edition, p. 149 and J.P. Barbier, *Bibliographie des Discours politiques de Ronsard,* Genève, 1984, p. 145 – 205.

(160) On the influence of Ronsard's *Discours,* see the introduction to my edition, p. 21 – 25.

(161) P.F. Geisendorf concluded that Bèze approved of the objective of the conspirators but not the means they used (*Théodore de Bèze,* Genève, 1949, p. 117 – 119).

(162) Lines 699–710; see my edition of his *Discours,* p. 188–189.

(163) The poem was said by contemporaries to have been written by Ronsard and Baïf in collaboration with Lancelot Carle. It is an adaptation of a song written in 1554 and attributed to Mellin de Saint-Gelais: see Ronsard, S.T.F.M., XVIII, p. 439–444 and 439, n. 1. In addition to the two manuscripts in the Bibliothèque Nationale noted there, a manuscript copy was made by a contemporary collector and annotator of Ronsard, Jean de Piochet: see Barbier, *Ma bibliothèque poétique, II, Ronsard,* p. 332–333 and V.-L. Saulnier, 'Autour du Colloque de Poissy: les avatars d'une chanson de Saint-Gelais à Ronsard et Théophile', *Bibliothèque d'Humanisme et Renaissance,* XX, 1958, p. 44–78.

(164) The editors of Bèze's *Correspondance* surmise (III, p. 237, n. 4) that it was at a place called Popincourt, in the Faubourg Saint-Antoine, that Ronsard heard Bèze preach. Self-evidently, Ronsard's intention was not to receive edification, but to observe and to comment — or, as his foes were to put it, to 'jazer' and 'moquer'. See his *Responce aux injures,* l. 719–740 (p. 189–190 in my edition of the *Discours*). Ronsard notes there that he was saved by his 'sourdesse benine' from imbibing any of Bèze's doctrine, and that his escape from the sermon resembled that of a shipwrecked merchant scrambling ashore while his companions drown.

(165) For example, Claude de Sainctes attacked 'Le capitaine Besze, ministre du Christ des Juifs empistolé, au lieu de Jesus des Chrestiens crucifié' (in his *Discours sur le saccagement des Eglises Catholiques,* Paris, 1562, B.L. 3901 cc 51, 71ro; see also 53ro, 63ro).

(166) See Geisendorf, *Théodore de Bèze,* p. 194, who observes that the massacre at Wassy had just demonstrated the Reformers' need for precautions.

(167) See Pineaux, *Polémique protestante,* p. 75 – 76 and 142 – 143.

(168) See the *Continuation du discours des miseres,* l. 95 – 143; p. 82 – 86 in my edition.

(169) See Pineaux, *Polémique protestante,* p. 79 – 80, 149, 390, 458 – 459.

(170) Evidence that this is an allusion to Bèze is presented in my edition, p. 110. The identification is corroborated by a contemporary annotator, Jean de Piochet: see Barbier, *Ma bibliothèque poétique, II, Ronsard,* p. 338.   J. Pineaux referred to this passage but missed the allusion (see his 'Poésie et prophétisme: Ronsard et Théodore de Bèze dans la querelle des *Discours', Revue d'histoire littéraire de la France,* LXXVIII, 1978 p. 531).

(171) See my edition, p. 134. We shall see later that Théodore Agrippa d'Aubigné, too, was to echo this passage — also, it seems, alluding to Ronsard.

(172) *Response,* l. 27, 490 (p. 156 and 179 in my edition). The further passages, with page references in my edition of the *Discours des miseres,* are the following. The Reformers are divided among themselves — 'Et bien tost s'ouvrira l'escole Beszienne' (p. 93). My ancestors (says Ronsard) are in paradise — 'Encor qu'ils n'aient suivy ny Calvin ny de Besze' (p. 109). A Latin poem published with the *P. Ronsardi Responsum* (which is probably by Jean Dorat), declares that Théodore de Bèze has the same view on theology as the ancient Theodore, that is, he is an atheist (p. 213).

(173) Echoes of Ronsard are found in Belleforest, Arnaud Sorbin, Florimond de Raemond and Bérulle: see the note in my edition of the *Discours* (p. 84).

(174) However, the possibility cannot be exluded that he did. A copy of Reformers' pamphlets against Ronsard, in the British Library, has a manuscript note to the effect that Bèze replied to Ronsard. The book, *Palinodies de Pierre de Ronsard* (1563;

B.L. C 132 h 10 (3)) has four lines presented as a poem and headed *Ronsard contre Bèze,* followed by another four lines titled *Bezze à Ronsard.* But the work attributed to Ronsard is simply four individual lines taken from different parts of Ronsard's *Discours.* I do not know the source of the material ascribed to Bèze, which begins 'Un capusson de fols', and which I am unable to decipher. It is quite possible that an as-yet unidentified reply by Bèze is among the many lost pamphlets against Ronsard. Ronsard gave a summary list of these pamphlets (see S.T.F.M., XII, p. 10, or my edition of the *Discours des miseres,* p. 223). P. Charbonnier's *Pamphlets protestants contre Ronsard, 1560–1577* (Paris, 1923) remains the definitive list, to which have to be added the two texts I published in *Bibliothèque d'Humanisme et Renaissance* (XXXVII, 1975, p. 73–86 and XLVIII, 1986, p. 421–430).

(175) Bèze was to publish Greek translations of the psalms by Chrestien in 1566, and, in the 1569 edition of his *Poemata,* an cpitaph of Calvin by him. See Gardy, *Bibliographie des œuvres de Bèze,* nos. 228 and 5 respectively.

(176) See the *Epistre* which prefaces Ronsard's *Recueil des nouvelles poesies* of 1564 (p. 225 in my edition of the *Discours*). The evidence that Chrestien is one of the two targets of this *epistre* is summarized in my edition, p. 224–225, 228.

(177) In his *Apologie d'un homme chrestien*: see Pineaux, *Polémique protestante,* p. 494–495.

(178) For the attribution of this text to Chrestien, see Pineaux, *Polémique protestante,* p. 326 and Barbier, *Ma Bibliothèque poétique, II, Ronsard,* p. 340. Text in Pineaux, *Polémique protestante,* p. 324–395.

(179) For the attribution of this text, see Pineaux, *Polémique protestante,* p. 462 and my edition of Ronsard's *Discours,* p. 224–225. The text of the *Apologie ou deffense* is in Pineaux, *Polémique protestante,* p. 460–502. We shall see later in this

chapter that Ronsard alleged that Chrestien, before his change of religion, had written against Bèze.

(180) Pineaux, *Polémique protestante,* p. 303–304. On Grévin's role, see K.J. Evans in 'Grévin, author of the *Temple de Ronsard?',* *Bibliothèque d'Humanisme et Renaissance,* XLVII, 1985, p. 619–625. The text of the *Temple* is in Pineaux, *Polémique protestante,* p. 300–323.

(181) This is suggested by Ronsard's allusions to one of his foes as a 'chrestien reformé' and a 'correcteur de livres' (Chrestien published editions of Greek texts): see the preface to *Le premier livre du Recueil des nouvelles poësies* of 1564 (p. 225 and 228 in my edition of his *Discours des miseres*).

(182) Taken from Pineaux, *Poésie des Protestants,* p. 27–28.

(183) See Barbier, *Ma Bibliothèque poétique, II, Ronsard,* p. 329–330 and 372–373. See also Pineaux in *Bulletin de la Société d'Histoire du protestantisme français,* 1983, p. 357–361. According to Laumonier (S.T.F.M. edition, X, p. 365, n. 2), the fact that Ronsard retained in successive editions of his works the poems dedicated to Des Masures, and the name of Des Masures, is a 'preuve que Des Masures n'a pas pris rang parmi les pamphlétaires huguenots de 1563, et qu'on lui a faussement attribué la *Replique* de D.M. Lescaldin'. Laumonier's reasoning is questionable, however: Ronsard might not have known of this *Replique,* and even if he did he might not have known who wrote it. The text of the *Replique* is in Pineaux, *Polémique protestante,* p. 228–229.

(184) The work was published in Geneva; I used the copy in the B.L. (698 c 4 (8), A ii^{vo}).

(185) Text taken from Bèze, *Correspondance,* VI, p. 317–319.

(186) Many references to Antoine de Chandieu, or La Roche-Chandieu, are found in Bèze's *Correspondance,* though the letters they exchanged are lost. Bèze attached importance to Chandieu's *Confirmation de la discipline ecclesiastique* of 1566: see his *Correspondance,* XIII, p. 31, 33, 109. He

published Chandieu's epitaph of Calvin in his 1569 *Poemata* (p. 130): see Gardy, *Bibliographie des œuvres de Théodore de Bèze*, no. 5, and cf. no. 6. In 1567, Chandieu published a refutation of a book by Claude de Sainctes against Calvin and Bèze (see Geisendorf, *Bèze*, p. 275, n. 3); and he is the probable author of French translations of poems by Bèze on the death of Coligny (see Pineaux, *Poésie des Protestants,* p. 157, n. 3). In 1581, he appears to have collaborated with Bèze and others in producing the *Harmonia confessionum fidei* (see Gardy, p. 184 – 185). In the 1597 edition of the *Poemata* (Gardy, no. 9), Bèze included an epitaph of Chandieu, and a new poem dedicated to him. On Chandieu, see A. Bernus, 'Le ministre Antoine de Chandieu d'après son journal autographe inédit (1534 – 1591)', in the *Bulletin* of the Société de l'Histoire du protestantisme français, XXXVII, 1888, p. 2 – 13, 57 – 69, 124 – 136, 169 – 191, 393 – 415, 449 – 462, 561 – 577, 617 – 635.

(187) The text of Zamariel's *Response* is in Pineaux, *Polémique protestante,* p. 28 – 50. Pineaux argued (p. 2) that the Reformers's *Palinodies* of Ronsard (parodies of his *Discours* which present the poet as saying the opposite of what he did say) were also by Chandieu, but with no real evidence; his view is based on the (dubious) assertion that Ronsard's *Responce,* which includes a passage deriding these *Palinodies,* was written exclusively against Chandieu.

(188) See Barbier, *Ma Bibliothèque poétique, II, Ronsard,* p. 194 and 308 – 309.

(189) See my edition of the *Discours,* p. 224 – 225, and R. Vergès, 'Ronsard et Florent Chrestien, à propos d'un sonnet anonyme', in *Mélanges offerts à Paul Laumonier,* Paris, 1935, p. 257 – 267.

(190) '[. . .] Sed eheu hæc est magna temporum nostrorum miseria et calamitas, ut Ronsardi Poëmata , quærimoniæ nescio quæ ad Regem, Reginam aut nescio quos homines, non tam cito nascantur quam edantur ab ipsis typographis. Disputa-

tiones autem veterum Theologorum et utilissimæ et optimæ et quæ faciunt ad mores spernantur [...]': quoted by P. de Felice, in *Lambert Daneau,* Paris, 1881, p. 273. Daneau was to become a close associate of Bèze after fleeing to Geneva at the time of the St Bartholomew's Day massacres: see Bèze, *Correspondance,* XVI, p. 209 and 211, n. 4 and Gardy, *Bibliographie des œuvres de Bèze,* p. 184–185.

(191) See S.T.F.M., XII, p. 172–188; XIII, p. 1–14, 15–29.

(192) See the unnumbered pages at the end of Sourdeval's edition.

(193) For the text, see George Buchanan's *Franciscanus et fratres, quibus accessere varia eiusdem et aliorum poëmata,* 3v., Basiliæ Rauracorum [1568], B.L. 1213 g 10, III, p. 84. On Utenhove's closeness to the Pléiade, see Nolhac, *Ronsard et l'humanisme,* p. 7, 67, 106, 170 n. 2, 174–176, 215–218 and 347–349. On his religion, see W. Janssen, *Charles Utenhove, sa vie et son œuvre (1536–1600),* Maastricht, 1939, p. 10–14, 22, 35, 46–49, 53–55, 60–61 (and p. 31–35 for a discussion of his link with Ronsard).

(194) *Discours contre Machiavel,* ed. A. D'Andrea and P.D. Stewart, Firenze, 1974, p. 78.

(195) See Ronsard, S.T.F.M., XV, p. 3–10.

(196) *Deux Dialogues du nouveau langage françois italianizé,* ed. P.M. Smith, Genève, 1980, p. 339–340.

(197) See my *Montaigne and the Roman Censors,* Genève, 1981, p.23–35.

(198) See *La Legende de Charles cardinal de Lorraine,* Reims, 1579, B.L. 804 a 2 (1), 20vo-21ro.

(199) Quoted from Pineaux, *Poésie des Protestants,* p. 383 and 55–56. In the latter case, Pineaux was quoting from a 1593 edition of this work.

(200) From *Les Tragiques,* ed. A. Garnier and J. Plattard, Paris, 1990, p. 69–70 (*Princes,* l. 949–956, 970). Ronsard's *Des vertus* is in S.T.F.M., XVIII, p. 451–460.

(201) The letter was written to accompany a presentation copy for the Queen of Ronsard's *Elegies, Mascarades et Bergerie* of 1565. I published the text in 'Ronsard and Queen Elizabeth I', *Bibliothèque d'Humanisme et Renaissance,* XXIX, 1967, p. 96, n. 18.

(202) See *Les Hymnes ecclesiastiques selon le cours de l'année, avec autres cantiques spirituelz,* second edition, Paris, 1582, B.L. 1074 a 13 (1, 2), a iii^{ro-vo}.

(203) See Ronsard, S.T.F.M., XIII, p. 261–264.

(204) I used the copy in the B.L., 640 k 3 (1); my quotation is from p. 248. Other relevant passages are on p. 24, 121, 189, 311 and 319. On Lefèvre de La Boderie, the orientalist and collaborator on the famous Antwerp polyglot Bible, see Rosanna Gorris's introduction to her edition of his *Diverses meslanges poetiques,* Genève, 1993.

(205) The relevant passage is in Ronsard, S.T.F.M., XIV, p. 196–197.

(206) See Ronsard, S.T.F.M., XII, p. 50.

(207) See Ronsard, S.T.F.M., XII, p. 71–72.

(208) See Ronsard, S.T.F.M., XIV, p. 4.

(209) There is a useful discussion of Ronsard's use of allegory in I. Silver, 'Ronsard's theory of allegory: the antinomy between myth and truth', *Kentucky Romance Quarterly,* XVIII, 1971 (p. 363–407), p. 394–403.

(210) See 'The hidden meaning of Ronsard's *Hymne de l'Hyver'*, in *French Renaissance Studies in honor of Isidore Silver,* ed. F.S. Brown (*Kentucky Romance Quarterly,* XXI, Supplement 2), 1974, p. 85–97.

(211) See Ronsard, S.T.F.M., XV, p. 178–185.

(212) See Ronsard, S.T.F.M., XVI, p. 10. Ronsard's biographer, Claude Binet, cited allegorical interpretations of the *Franciade* which he said Ronsard pointed out to him (see *La Vie de P. de Ronsard,* ed. P. Laumonier, Paris, 1910, variant C).

(213) See S.T.F.M., XVIII, p. 97 – 98.

(214) This interpretation is found in *Dialogue auquel sont traitées plusieurs choses advenues aux Lutheriens et Huguenots de la France* of 1573 (which is better known by the title under which it was reissued in the following year: *Le Reveille-matin des François et de leurs voisins, composé par Eusebe Philadelphe, cosmopolite*). See N. Cazauran, 'La «Tragique peinture» du premier dialogue du *Réveille-matin'*, in *Etudes seiziémistes offertes à V.-L. Saulnier,* Genève, 1980 (p. 327 – 346), p. 336 – 338.

(215) In his *Altera apologia* to Sainctes, Bèze wrote: ' Poeticos meos lusus quum ut res serio dictas et scriptas interpretaris, quis te judex æquus audiat? [. . .] Testor et illud, tam fictitiam esse Publiam illam [. . .] quam est vester panaceus Deus[. . .] Et quænam illa est Candida? ' (cited by Pineaux, *Polémique protestante,* p. 79, n. to l. 284, from Bèze's *Volumen [. . .] tractationum theologicarum,* Genève, 1582, II, p. 359 – 360).

(216) Referring to poetry, Bèze says:

> [. . .] quod studiorum genus, quum iam pridem certo animi judicio, quod mihi juveni multa neque recte cogitata neque christiane scripta excidissent, prorsus omisissem repetere me tandem, animi relaxandi causa, coegit ista maledicorum quorundam improbitas, qui mores meos ex fictis istis lusibus idcirco metiuntur, quod alioqui, Dei gratia, nihil aliud inveniunt, quod in anteacta vita mea probabiliter reprehendant; neque interea vident, se illa in me reprehendere, quæ in aliis virtuti ducant. Quis enim eorum, qui apud ipsos poeticen colunt, aliter scripsit? Spero autem me et hæc et alia putidissima mendacia ita refutaturum, ut et bonis omnibus satisfiat, si qui fortasse nonnihil inde malæ de me suspicionis hauserunt; et om-

nis istiusmodi convitiorum turpitudo in ipsorum caput redundet.

(*Correspondance,* IX, p. 146).

(217) On Dudithius's links with Dorat and Ronsard, see P. de Nolhac, *Ronsard et l'humanisme,* Paris, 1966, p. 210 – 211.

(218) Cited from the 1569 edition (B.L. 677 b 23), p. 12 – 14; another 1569 edition in the B.L. has 'sic enim potius arbitrari volo' in l. 8 of the quotation. The text is also in Bèze's *Correspondance,* X, p. 88 – 100; the passage I have cited is on p. 92.

(219) See the interesting and important notes in Bèze's *Correspondance.* A rejoinder to this passage was to be published in 1583 by Bénigne Poissenot in *L'Esté,* who defends the *Amadis* novels and refutes Bèze's condemnation of 'deux hommes les plus singuliers en leur profession que ce siecle ait porté', i.e. Ronsard and Du Bellay (ed. G.A. Pérouse, M. Simonin, D. Baril, Genève, 1987, p. 213 – 214).

(220) See Gardy, *Bibiographie des œuvres de Bèze,* no. 6.

(221) Gardy does not include this work among those of Bèze, but notes 'Ainsi que l'a établi Giesendorf (p. 340s.), cette histoire a été compilée en partie avec des matérieux que Bèze prenait soin de réunir dès 1565, et le travail de compilation semble s'être déroulé à Genève, sous sa haute direction; mais Bèze n'a jamais cessé d'en parler, dans sa correspondance, comme d'une œuvre anonyme' (*Bibliographie,* p. 222).

(222) *Histoire ecclesiastique des Eglises Réformées de France,* éd. G. Baum, E. Cunitz, 3 t., Paris, 1883 – 89, II, p. 633 – 634 (II, p. 538 – 539 in the original edition).

(223) The passage in the *Remonstrance à la Royne* is in Pineaux, *Polémique protestante,* p. 137. Stories that Ronsard was involved in the Saint-Calais massacres have won wide acceptance, but I am sceptical because (a) the passage in this *Remonstrance* merely says Ronsard hoped to get his hand on

some of the spoils, and may or may not have known of the planned massacre — in other words, it insinuates without evidence; (b) none of the other extant contemporary pamphlets against him mentions anything of the sort, and if there had been substance to such episodes the Reformers would have exploited them to discredit Ronsard's ironies about Bèze's *evangile armée*; (c) this first clear account of Ronsard's armed clash with Reformers (as distinct from insinuation) surfaces eighteen years after the event in a publication hostile to Ronsard (the *Histoire ecclesiastique*); (d) Louis Froger pointed out that Ronsard was not in the area at the time (*Ronsard et la Réforme*, 1904, p. 287; and see his 'Ronsard et les Vêpres calaisiennes', *Annales Fléchoises,* VIII, p. 366 – 370); and (e) if there were any substance to these stories, Ronsard could not safely have claimed, as he did, to be free of sectarianism and violence (see S.T.F.M., XII, p. 15, 181).

(224) Text cited from the anthology at the end of the *Poemata,* 1582 (Geneva, B.L. 1213 f 5), titled *Carmina quæ ad eius poemata antea excusa accesserunt,* a v^{ro-vo}. Gardy does not include the 1582 edition in his *Bibliographie des œuvres de Théodore de Bèze.* The poem reappeared in the 1597 edition of the *Poemata* with the title *In poetarum nomine abutentes* (B.L. 837 i 3, p. 62 – 63). There is another denunciation of erotic verse at the beginning of Bèze's *Sylva III* (*Natalia domini*), p. 74 in the same edition.

(225) See Jacques-Davy Du Perron, *Oraison funebre sur le mort de Monsieur de Ronsard (1586),* ed. M. Simonin, Genève, 1985, p. 87 – 90 and notes; F.A. Yates, *The French Academies of the Sixteenth Century,* reprint, London and New York, 1988, chap. ix, 'The funeral of Ronsard', p. 177 – 198; and, for the durability of Ronsard's reputation, J. Dagens, 'Ronsard et l'*Histoire catholique* d'Hilarion de Coste', *Mélanges Chamard,* Paris, 1951, p. 145 – 151 and his *Bérulle et les origines de la restauration catholique (1575 – 1611)* [Paris, 1952,] p. 59 – 65.

(226) See J. Velliardus, *Petri Ronsardi poetæ gallici laudatio funebris,* Parisiis, 1586, B.N. Ln^{27} 17840, 16^{ro-vo}.

(227) Either Crichton had not read the *Folastries* or, as a propagandist, he was very free of inhibitions about the truth. The text in the original is as follows:

> Damnatur unum illud in eius operibus quod amatoria quædam conscripserit: quasi vero ista hominis et non ætatis sint vitia, et non omnibus poëtis in adolescentia effundente sese paulo liberius ingenii vena non quædam sint resecanda: qui tamen amorum libri quid habent quod non in puellarum choro legi possit? Num lasciva ulla aut paulo inverecundior linea? Certe nulla: utinam isti qui hæc loquuntur tam de Catholicis sacris mererentur quam is qui hac contumeliæ nota citra ullam ipsius culpam aspergitur.

(G. Crittonius, *Laudatio funebris, habita in exequiis Petri Ronsardi apud Becodianos, cui præponuntur eiusdem Ronsardi carmina partim a moriente, partim a languente dictata,* Lutetiæ, 1586, B.N. Ln^{27} 17841, p. 7).

(228) See Jung, *Hercule dans la littérature,* p. 121.

(229) See R.A. Katz, *Ronsard's French Critics, 1585–1828,* Genève, 1966, p. 38–39.

(230) The two hymns are the *Hynne des Peres de famille à Monsieur S. Blaise* and the *Hynne de Monsieur Sainct Roch* (S.T.F.M., XVIII, p. 275–280 and 280–282).

(231) 'Il avoit envie, si la santé et la Parque l'eussent permis, d'escrire plusieurs œuvres Chrestiennes, et traiter ingenieusement et dignement la naissance du monde; mais il nous en a laissé seulement le desir' (Ronsard, S.T.F.M., XVIII, p. 293).

(232) See Pineaux, *Poésie des Protestants,* p. 324, 327. For an earlier example of poems by Catholics in a Reformers' *chansonnier,* see Pineaux, p. 296–297.

(233) 'Il faut croire que les vieilles haines comme les anciennes exclusives disparaissaient peu à peu' (Pineaux, *Poésie des Protestants,* p. 331).

(234) From the preface to Richeome's *Tableaux sacrez des figures mystiques du tres-auguste sacrifice et sacrement de l'Eucharistie* (Paris, 1601, B.L. 4323 bb 48 (1)), p. 8.

(235) See my edition, published by Medieval and Renaissance Studies and Texts (Binghamton, New York), 1994.

(236) Aubigné records, in a famous letter on the poets of his age, that when he was twenty he sent some of his poems to Ronsard who replied to him, and that this was the start of a personal acquaintanceship. In the same letter, he speaks glowingly of Ronsard: 'Je vous convie et ceux qui me croiront, à lire et relire ce poëte sur tous. C'est luy qui a coupé le filet que la France avoit soubs la langue' (quoted, from his *Œuvres complètes,* ed. E. Réaume, F. de Caussade, Paris, 1873 – 1892, I, p. 457, by Katz, in *Ronsard's French Critics,* p. 33).

(237) See Pineaux, *Poésie de Protestants,* p. 336, 343, 344.

(238) See his *Response aux injures,* lines 13 – 16, 59 – 62 and especially 1019 – 1042 (p. 155 – 156, 158 and 203 – 205 in my edition).

(239) In the preface, Ronsard includes Chrestien in a list of 'divines testes et sacrées aux Muses' (S.T.F.M., XVI, p. 351). On the reconciliation between them, see S.T.F.M., XVIII, p. 496 and note.

(240) See Nolhac, *Un Poète rhénan ami de la Pléiade, Paul Melissus,* Paris, 1923, p. 89 – 93. Nolhac observed (p. 223 – 224) that it was to Florent Chrestien that Melissus sent his ode for the memorial volume on Ronsard's death.

(241) Montaigne relates his many courteous encounters with Reformers in his *Journal de voyage.*

Bibliography

(i) Primary sources

Théodore de BÈZE, *Les Juvenilia. Texte latin complet, avec la traduction des Epigrammes et des epitaphes, et des recherches sur la querelle des Juvenilia*, par A. Machard, Paris, 1879; reprint Genève, 1970.

Théodore de BÈZE, *Correspondance*, ed. H. Aubert, F. Aubert, H. Meylan *et al.* (Travaux d'Humanisme et Renaissance), Genève, 1960 onwards, vols. 1–16.

Théodore de BÈZE, *Poemata*, 1548, Lutetiæ, B.L. 11403 aaa 35.

Théodore de BÈZE, *Poemata*, 1569, B.L. 677 b 23.

Théodore de BÈZE, *Carmina*, [1588,] [includes a poem addressed to him by Des Masures, titled *Consilium*; cf. Bèze, *Correspondance*, XV, p. ix].

Théodore de BÈZE, *Abraham sacrifiant*, ed. K. Cameron, K.M. Hall, F. Higman (T.L.F.), Genève, 1967.

Théodore de BÈZE, *Psaumes mis en vers français (1551–1562), accompagnés de la version en prose de Loïs Budé*, ed. P. Pidoux, Genève, 1984.

129

Théodore de BÈZE: see also MAROT.

Claude BINET, *La Vie de P. de Ronsard,* ed. P. Laumonier, Paris, 1910.

Jérôme BOLSEC, *Histoire de la vie, mœurs et deportements de Théodore de Bèze,* Paris, 1577, B.L. 701 a 47.

Chansons tressalutaires et catholiques pour les bons chrestiens, à l'honneur de Dieu et de nostre mere saincte Eglise, Rouen, 1554, B.L. 11475 a 8.

Guillaume COLLETET, *Vie d'Etienne Dolet,* ed. M. Magnien (T.L.F.), Genève, 1992.

Jean CALVIN, *Opera quæ supersunt omnia,* ed. G. Baum, E. Cunitz, E. Reuss and continuators, 59 v., 1863 – 1900 (*Corpus Reformatorum,* 19 – 87), t. 12, for his letters.

Guillaume COLLETET, *Pierre de Ronsard,* ed. F.B. Caldari, Paris, 1983.

Louis DES MASURES, *Vingt pseaumes de David traduits selon la verité hebraïque et mis en rime françoise,* Lion, 1557, B.Nat. Rés. Ye 368 and 419.

Louis DES MASURES, *Tragédies saintes: David combattant, David triomphant, David fugitif,* ed. C. Comte, Paris, 1932.

Jean DORAT, *Poëmatia,* Lutetiæ, 1586, B.L. 1070 d 28.

Joachim DU BELLAY, *L'Olive,* ed. E. Caldarini (T.L.F.), Genève, 1974.

Joachim DU BELLAY, *La Monomachie de David et de Goliath,* ed. E. Caldarini (T.L.F.), Genève, 1981.

Joachim DU BELLAY, *Œuvres poétiques,* ed. H. Chamard (v. 1 – 6), G. Demerson (v. 7, 8) (S.T.F.M.), 8 v., Paris, 1908 – 85.

Joachim DU BELLAY, *La Deffence et illustration de la langue françoyse,* ed. H. Chamard, Paris (S.T.F.M.), 1948.

Jacques-Davy DU PERRON, *Oraison funebre sur le mort de Monsieur de Ronsard (1586)*, ed. M. Simonin (T.L.F.), Genève, 1985.

Histoire ecclesiastique des Eglises Réformées de France, ed. G. Baum, E. Cunitz, 3 t., Paris, 1883–89.

Hymne à Dieu, pour la delivrance des François de la plus que Egyptienne servitude, en laquelle ils ont esté detenus par le passé, [s.l.,] [s.d.,] B. Nat. Ye 24330.

Estienne JODELLE, *Œuvres complètes*, ed. E. Balmas, 2 v., Paris, 1965, 1968.

Guy Lefèvre de LA BODERIE, *Diverses meslanges poetiques*, ed. R. Gorris (T.L.F.), Genève, 1993.

Guy Lefèvre de LA BODERIE, *Les Hymnes ecclesiastiques selon le cours de l'année, avec autres cantiques spirituelz*, second edition, Paris, 1582, B.L. 1074 a 13 (1,2).

Guy Lefèvre de LA BODERIE, *L'encyclie des secrets de l'eternité*, Anvers, [1570,] B.L. 640 k 3 (1).

Estienne de LA BOËTIE, *Œuvres complètes*, ed. L. Desgraves, 2 v., Bordeaux, 1991.

Antoine de LA FAYE, *De vita et obitu Theodori Bezæ Vezelii, ecclesiastæ et sacrarum litterarum professoris*, Genevæ, 1606, B.L. 489 g 20 (1) (and French translation by A. Teissier, 1681, B.L. 4867 a 10).

Jacobus LAINGAEUS, *De vita et moribus T. Bezæ*, Parisiis, 1585, B.L. 862 e 27 (1).

LAURENT, *Oratio de clarissimi theologi Bezæ obitu*, 1616.

Clément MAROT, *Les Psaumes*, ed. S.J. Lenselink, Assen, Kassel, 1969.

Clément MAROT, Théodore de BÈZE, *Les Psaumes en vers français avec leurs mélodies*, ed. P. Pidoux (T.L.F.), Genève, 1986.

Bernard de MONTMÉJA, *Poemes chrestiens de B. de Montméja et autres divers auteurs recueillis et nouvellement mis en lumiere par Philippes Depas,* [s.l.,] 1574, B.Nat. Rés. Ye 1825.

Estienne PASQUIER, *Les Recherches de la France,* Paris, 1611, B.L. 596 g 4.

Estienne PASQUIER, *Les Lettres,* Paris, 1586, B.L. 636 i 21.

Jacques PELETIER, *L'Art poetique,* ed. A. Boulanger, Paris, 1930.

Jacques PELETIER, *In Euclidis elementa geometrica demonstrationum libri sex,* Lugduni, 1557, B.L. 8548 f 20.

Jacques PELETIER, *Œuvres poetiques,* Paris, 1547, B.L. 240 e 6 (reprint by M. Françon, Rochecorbon, 1958).

Jacques PELETIER, *Œuvres poetiques,* ed. L. Séché, P. Laumonier, Paris, 1904.

J. PINEAUX, *ed., La Polémique protestante contre Ronsard* (S.T.F.M.), Paris, 1973.

Louis RICHEOME, *Tableaux sacrez des figures mystiques du tres-auguste sacrifice et sacrement de l'Eucharistie,* Paris, 1601, B.L. 4323 bb 48 (1).

André de RIVAUDEAU, *Œuvres poétiques,* ed. C. Nourain de Sourdeval, Paris, 1859.

Pierre de RONSARD, *Œuvres complètes,* ed. P. Laumonier, I. Silver, R. Lebègue (S.T.F.M.), 20 v., Paris, 1914–75.

Pierre de RONSARD, *Discours des miseres de ce temps,* ed. M. Smith (T.L.F.), Genève, 1979.

(ii) Historical studies

F. Aubert, J. Boussard, H. Meylan, 'Un premier recueil de poésies latines de Théodore de Bèze', *Bibliothèque d'Humanisme et Renaissance,* XV, 1953, p. 161 – 191, 258 – 294.

H.M. Baird, *Théodore de Bèze, the Counsellor of the French Reformation 1519 – 1605,* New York, 1899.

E. Balmas, 'G. Guéroult traducteur des psaumes', *Revue d'Histoire littéraire de la France,* LXVII, 1967, p. 705 – 725.

F.L. Battles, 'The theologian as poet: some remarks about the "found" poetry of John Calvin', in *From Faith to Faith: in honor of D.G. Miller,* ed. D.Y. Hadidian, Pittsburgh, 1979, p. 299 – 337.

J.P. Barbier, *Ma Bibliothèque poétique, II, Ronsard,* Genève, 1990.

W. Baum, *Theodor Beza,* 2 v., Leipzig, 1843, 1851; suppl., 1852.

Y. Bellenger, *Du Bellay, ses «Regrets» qu'il fit dans Rome,* Paris, 1975.

A. Bernus, *Théodore de Bèze à Lausanne,* Lausanne, 1900.

A. Bernus, 'Le ministre Antoine de Chandieu d'après son journal autographe inédit (1534 – 1591)', *Bulletin de la Société de l'Histoire du protestantisme français,* XXXVII, 1888, p. 2 – 13, 57 – 69, 124 – 136, 169 – 191, 393 – 415, 449 – 462, 561 – 577, 617 – 635.

Bibliographie internationale de l'Humanisme et de la Renaissance: Combed for Ronsard entries, to 1987.

D. Boccassini, *La parola riscritta: Guillaume Gueroult, poeta e traduttore nella Francia della Riforma,* Firenze, 1985.

C. Borgeaud, *Histoire de l'Université de Genève,* 1900.

T.C. Cave, *Devotional Poetry in France, c. 1570 – 1613,* Cambridge, England, 1969.

H. Chamard, 'L'invention de l'ode et le différend de Ronsard et de Du Bellay', *Revue d'Histoire Littéraire de la France,* VI, 1899, p. 21–54.

H. Chamard, *Joachim Du Bellay, 1522–1560,* Lille, 1900.

H. Chamard, *Histoire de la Pléiade,* 4 v., Paris, 1939–1940.

F. Charbonnier, *Pamphlets protestants contre Ronsard, 1560–1577,* Paris, 1923.

F. Charbonnier, *La Poésie française et les guerres de religion (1560–1574),* reprint, Genève, 1970.

M. Chopard, 'Louis Des Masures en Lorraine: une source de l'*Histoire des martyrs* de Crespin', *Mélanges V.L. Saulnier,* ed. P.G. Castex, Genève, 1984 p. 629–639.

R.J. Clements, *Critical Theory and Practice of the Pléiade,* reprint, New York, 1970.

P. Costil, *André Dudith, humaniste hongrois, 1553–1589,* Paris, 1935.

J. Dagens, 'Ronsard et l'*Histoire catholique* d'Hilarion de Coste', *Mélanges offerts à Henri Chamard,* Paris, 1951, p. 145–151.

N.Z. Davis, 'Peletier and Beza part company', *Studies in the Renaissance,* XI, 1964, p. 188–222.

G. Demerson, *La Mythologie classique dans l'œuvre lyrique de la Pléiade,* Genève, 1972.

O. Douen, *Clément Marot et le psautier huguenot,* 2 v., reprint, Amsterdam, 1967 (original edition Paris, 1878).

E. Doumergue, *Jean Calvin, les hommes et les choses de son temps,* 7 v., Lausanne, Neuilly/S., 1899–1927.

A. Dufour, 'La définition de l'Église: un dialogue entre Dudith et Bèze', *Musée Neuchâtelois,* 1982, no. 4, p. 207–214.

S. Eckhardt, *Rémy Belleau,* Budapest, 1917.

M. Engamarre, *'Qu'il me baise des baisiers de sa bouche': le Cantique des Cantiques à la Renaissance*, Genève, 1993.

P. de Felice, *Lambert Daneau*, Paris, 1881.

L. Froger, *Ronsard et la réforme*, 1904.

G. Gadoffre, *Du Bellay et le sacré*, Paris, 1978.

F. Gardy, *Bibliographie des œuvres théologiques, littéraires, historiques et juridiques de Théodore de Bèze*, Genève, 1960.

P.F. Geisendorf, *Théodore de Bèze*, Genève, 1949.

A.L. Gordon, *Ronsard et la rhétorique*, Genève, 1970.

F. Higman, *'Chantez au Seigneur un nouveau cantique:* le Psautier de Genève au XVIe siècle', *Lumière et Vie*, CCII, 1991, p. 25–39.

M. Jeanneret, *Poésie et tradition biblique au XVIe siècle: recherches stylistiques sur les paraphrases des psaumes de Marot à Malherbe*, Paris, 1969.

C. Jugé, *Jacques Peletier du Mans (1517–1582)*, Paris, Le Mans, 1907.

M.R. Jung, *Hercule dans la littérature française du XVIe siècle*, Genève, 1960.

M. Jurgens, *ed., Ronsard et ses amis, documents du Minutier Central des notaires de Paris*, Paris, Archives nationales, 1985.

R.A. Katz, *Ronsard's French Critics, 1585–1828*, Genève, 1966.

O. Klapp, *Bibliographie der französische Literaturwissenschaft*, Frankfurt, 1960 onwards.

P. Laumonier, *Ronsard poète lyrique*, 2e éd., Paris, 1923.

Robin A. Leaver, *'Goostly psalmes and spirituall songes': English and Dutch metrical psalms from Coverdale to Uten-*

hove, 1535–1566, New York and Oxford, Clarendon Press, 1991.

K. Ley, 'Calvins Kritik an Ronsard', in A. Buck, ed., *Renaissance–Reformation, Gegensätze und Gemeinsamkeiten,* Wiesbaden, 1984, p. 105–129.

H. de Lubac, *Exégèse médiévale: les quatre sens de l'Ecriture,* 4 v., Paris, 1959–1964.

C. Maddison, *Apollo and the Nine, a History of the Ode,* London, 1960.

D. Ménager, *Ronsard: le roi, le poète et les hommes,* Genève, 1979.

H. Meylan, 'La conversion de Bèze ou les longues hésitations d'un humaniste chrétien', in his *D'Erasme à Théodore de Bèze,* Genève, 1987, p. 145–167.

A. Moss, *Poetry and Fable: Studies in Mythological Narrative in Sixteenth-century France,* Cambridge, England, etc., 1984.

P. de Nolhac, *Un Poète rhénan ami de la Pléiade, Paul Melissus,* Paris, 1923.

P. de Nolhac, *Ronsard et l'humanisme,* Paris, 1921; reprint, Paris, 1966.

P. Pidoux, *Le Psautier huguenot du XVIe siècle,* 2 v., Bâle, 1962.

J. Pineaux, *La Poésie des protestants de langue française (1559–1589),* Paris, 1971.

J. Pineaux, 'Poésie et prophétisme: Ronsard et Théodore de Bèze dans la querelle des *Discours*', *Revue d'Histoire Littéraire de la France,* LXXVIII, 1978, p. 531–540.

J. Pineaux, 'De Ronsard à Ovide: un humaniste protestant devant la poésie d'amour' [André de Rivaudeau], *Bulletin de la Société de l'Histoire du Protestantisme Français*, CXXVII, 1982, p. 477–492.

J. Pineaux, 'Louis Des Masures et Jean de Tournes dans la querelle des *Discours*', *Bulletin de la Société de l'Histoire du Protestantisme Français*, CXXVIII, 1983, p. 357–361.

A.L. Prescott, 'English writers and Beza's Latin epigrams', *Studies in the Renaissance*, XXI, 1974, p. 83–117.

A. Py, A. Dufour, J.P. Barbier, *Ronsard et la Rome protestante*, Genève, 1985.

M. Raymond, 'Deux pamphlets inconnus contre Ronsard et la Pléiade', *Revue du seizième siècle*, XIII, 1926, p. 243–264.

M. Raymond, 'Jean Tagaut, poète français et bourgeois de Genève', *Revue du seizième siècle*, XII, 1925.

M. Raymond, *L'Influence de Ronsard sur la poésie française (1550–1585)*, nouv. éd., Genève, 1965, chap. XIII, 'La doctrine de Ronsard et les poètes chrétiens', p. 329–357.

M. Richter, 'La poetica di Théodore de Bèze e le *Chrestiennes méditations*', *Aevum*, XXXVIII, 1964, p. 479–525.

M. Richter, *Jean de Sponde e la lingua poetica dei protestanti nel cinquecento*, Milano, 1973.

J. Seznec, *The Survival of the Pagan Gods*, New York, 1953.

I. Silver, 'Ronsard, the theological reaction, and the creation of a national poetic language', *L'Esprit créateur*, X, 1970, p. 95–103.

I. Silver, 'Ronsard's ethical thought', *Bibliothèque d'Humanisme et Renaissance*, XXIV, 1962, p. 88–117, 339–374.

I. Silver, 'Ronsard's theory of allegory: the antinomy between myth and truth', *Kentucky Romance Quarterly*, XVIII, 1971, p. 363–407.

M. Simon, *Hercule et le christianisme*, Paris, 1955.

138

M. Simonin, 'Les relations de Des Masures avec Dorat et Ronsard', *Bulletin du Bibliophile*, I, 1990, p. 63 – 88.

M. Simonin, 'L'apothéose de Ronsard dans l'*Oraison funèbre* de Du Perron', *Renaissance and Reformation / Renaissance et Réforme*, XI, 1987, p. 67 – 76.

M. Simonin, *Pierre de Ronsard*, Paris, 1990.

M. Simonin, 'La disgrâce d'Amadis', *Studi francesi*, LXXXII, 1984, p. 1 – 35.

M.C. Smith, 'Ronsard et ses critiques contemporains', in *Ronsard en son quatrième centenaire*, ed. Y. Bellenger *et al.*, Genève, 1988, p. 83 – 90.

M.C. Smith, 'Théodore de Bèze and Philænus', *Bibliothèque d'Humanisme et Renaissance*, LII, 1990, p. 345 – 353.

M.C. Smith, 'Joachim Du Bellay défenseur d'Etienne Dolet', in K.A. Kuczynski, Z.J. Nowak and H. Tadeusiewicz, eds., *Munera philologica Georgio Starnowski ab amicis collegis discipulis oblata*, Lódz, 1992, p. 141 – 147.

M.C. Smith, *Joachim Du Bellay's Veiled Victim*, Genève, 1974.

M.C. Smith, 'Opium of the people: Numa Pompilius in the French Renaissance', *Bibliothèque d'Humanisme et Renaissance*, LII, 1990, p. 7 – 21.

M.C. Smith, 'A lost Protestant pamphlet against Ronsard', *Bibliothèque d'Humanisme et Renaissance*, XXXVII, 1975, p. 73 – 86.

M.C. Smith, 'A Reformer's reply to Ronsard's *Discours à la Royne*', *Bibliothèque d'Humanisme et Renaissance*, XLVIII, 1986, 421 – 430.

M.C. Smith, 'The hidden meaning of Ronsard's *Hymne de l'Hyver*', in *French Renaissance Studies in honor of Isidore Silver*, ed. F.S. Brown, *Kentucky Romance Quarterly*, XXI, Supplement 2, 1974, p. 85 – 97.

T. Thomson, 'The *Poemata* of Théodore de Bèze', in I.D. McFarlane, *ed., Acta Conventus neo-Latini Sanctandreani*, Binghamton, New York, 1986, p. 409–415.

G.H. Tucker, *The Poet's Odyssey: Joachim Du Bellay and the* Antiquitez de Rome, Oxford, 1990.

R. Vergès, 'Ronsard et Florent Chrestien, à propos d'un sonnet anonyme', in *Mélanges offerts à Paul Laumonier*, Paris, 1935, p. 257–267.

D.P. Walker, *The Ancient Theology, Studies in Christian Platonism from the Fifteenth to the Eighteenth Century*, London, 1972.

J. Vignes, 'Paraphrase et appropriation: les avatars poétiques de l'*Ecclésiaste* au temps des guerres de religion (Dalbiac, Carle, Belleau, Baïf)', *Bibliothèque d'Humanisme et Renaissance*, LV, 1993, p. 503–526.

L. Wenceslaus, *L'Esthétique de Calvin*, reprint, Genève, 1979.

F. Wendel, *Calvin et l'humanisme*, Paris, 1976.

F.A. Yates, *The French Academies of the Sixteenth Century*, London and New York, 1988

Index Nominum

Aubigné, Théodore Agrippa d', 72-73, 90
Audebert, Germain, 100

Babinot, Albert, 29, 35-36, 70
Badius, Conrad, 13
Baïf, Jean-Antoine de, 74, 83
Binet, Claude, 88, 124

Calvin, Jean, 22, 30-31, 51, 68, 81
Carle, Lancelot, 117
Chrestien, Florent, 57-58, 63-64, 69, 90, 101
Courcelles, Pierre de, 58-59
Crichton, George, 86

Dalbiac, Accace, 29-30
Dampierre, Jean de, 46
Daneau, Lambert, 69-70
Danès, Pierre, 14
Daniel, Pierre, 69
Denisot, Nicolas, 28, 34, 107
Denosse, Catherine, 16
Des Autels, Guillaume, 55
Des Masures, Louis, 50-55, 65-67, 90

Desportes, Philippe, 72
Dolet, Estienne, 15-16, 21
Dorat, Jean, 74, 79, 97, 100
Du Bellay, Jean, 15, 37
Du Bellay, René, 11
Du Chastel, Pierre, 14
Dudycz, Andrea, 79-80

Escorbiac, Jean d', 87
Estienne, Henri, 72, 80, 81

Farel, Guillaume, 51
Foix, Paul de, 50, 73

Gentillet, Innocent, 71
Grévin, Jacques, 64
Gueroult, Guillaume, 30-31

Herberay des Essarts, Nicolas de, 23, 82
Heroët, Antoine, 18

Jodelle, Estienne, 27-28

La Boëtie, Estienne de, 35
La Haye, Robert de, 56-57, 67
La Noue, Odet de, 90

La Roche-Chandieu, Antoine de, 67-68
'Lavianus', 45
Lefèvre de La Boderie, Guy, 73-74
L'Hospital, Michel de, 25, 35, 45, 50
L'Huillier, Estienne, 88
L'Isle, François de, 72
Lorraine, Jean, Cardinal de, 50-53

Macer, Jean, 35
Macrin, Salmon, 97
Marnef, Enguilbert de, 31-32
Marot, Clément, 17-19, 22-23, 32, 41, 51, 55, 57, 72
Martin, Jean, 12
Marullus, Michael, 83
Melissus: see Schede
Monluc, Jean de, 14, 50, 74
Montaigne, Michel de, 59, 72, 73, 86-87, 90
Muret, Marc-Antoine, 34

Nicolaï, Nicolas de, 16

Olivier, François, 14

Paschal, Pierre, 55
Pasquier, Estienne, 14, 35, 98, 99

Peletier du Mans, Jacques, 11-14, 16, 18, 21, 31-34, 50, 54, 89
Poissenot, Bénigne, 125
Popon, Maclou, 97
Possevino, Antonio, 86

Rabelais, François, 76-77
Richeome, Louis, 89
Rivaudeau, André de, 36, 70
Rouspeau, Yves, 41-42, 72

Sainctes, Claude de, 79
Saint-Gelais, Mellin de, 18, 117
Sauvage, Denis, 92
Scève, Maurice, 14, 18, 83
Schede, Paul (Melissus), 55, 90
Spenser, Edmund, 90

Tagaut, Jean, 29
Tyard, Pontus de, 74

Utenhove, Charles, 70

Vascosan, Michel de, 12-13
Vauquelin de La Fresnaye, Jean, 74
Volmar, Melchior, 14, 16, 45-48

ACHEVÉ D'IMPRIMER
SUR LES PRESSES
DE L'IMPRIMERIE MÉDECINE ET HYGIÈNE
À GENÈVE (SUISSE)
JUILLET 1995